Mountain Bike Anchorage

Rosemary Austin

Mountain Bike Anchorage

ISBN 0-9764453-0-1

Published by
Near Point Press
7005 Apollo Court
Anchorage, AK 99504

Visit www.nearpointpress.com for photographs and trail updates.

Edited by Leon Unruh
Maps by Ian Moore, Alaska Map Science
Design and typesetting by Regina McConkey

Printed in the United States of America by:
A.T. Publishing and Printing, Inc.
1720 Abbott Road
Anchorage, AK 99507

Front cover photo:
Cover map courtesy of USGS.
Early fall ride in Russian Jack Springs Park by Rosemary Austin.

Back cover photos, from the top:
Winter riding on Eklutna Lake by Michael Dinneen Photography (www.dinneenphoto.com); Late winter ice biking in Far North Bicentennial Park by Jon Kunesh; Summer race in Kincaid Park by Michael Dinneen; Early October ride on the Powerline Trail by Rosemary Austin.

Author's Notes

In researching this guide, I experienced the wonder of discovering Anchorage all over again. I rode routes I hadn't been on in a few years, pedaled down paths I had passed by many times. I slowed down to look deeper into the forest and up slopes to spot wildlife. A few times I encountered black bears with their cubs on the trails. I tried to negotiate with moose so they would choose another path. To think that all this could happen within miles of my front door reminds me of why I live in Alaska. Contrary to the popular expression, Alaska is right here in the largest city. We need only venture out to explore.

My thanks goes out to all my biking friends who trusted me to lead them into and out of the woods on many occasions. To the people who work behind the scenes for our municipal and state parks and the BLM so that we may have our parks and trails to enjoy; to the visionaries who, as the city grew, have worked to assure that we could have these parks; to all the people who patiently answered my questions about our local trails and provided maps to guide me—thank you.

I want to thank each customer at Paramount Cycles who over the years asked me what trails I would recommend. You and the Wombats provided much of the inspiration for this book. To Lynn and Art for reading the early draft of the manuscript and making thoughtful comments while urging me on in this project; to those who joined me on some of the research rides and stood waiting as I wrote notes or took photos—thanks.

For Bill Sherwonit and the writing workshop participants at Across the Bay Tent and Breakfast, for providing thoughtful comments and the inspiration to help me finish this project; for my editor, Leon, and mapmaker, Ian, for your work in helping to fulfill my vision—thanks.

Finally, thanks to Jon for sharing your passion for cycling and encouraging me to pursue my goal of writing this guide for our fellow mountain bikers.

All links in the chain, I offer my sincere gratitude.

January, 2005

Caution:

Trails change.
Crashes happen.
People get lost.

Bicycling can be dangerous whether you're in the city or on mountain trails. Hazards include bears, moose, rocks, steep hills, cold weather, motor vehicles and other trail users, including other bikers. The author, editor, publisher, mapmaker and printer are not responsible for accidents that occur while using this guide. Riders using this book accept all responsibility for any injuries—or worse—that may occur on any route presented in this book.

Contents

Legend

⌒‿⌒	Narrow Unpaved Trail
⌒‿·	Wide Unpaved Trail
∿	Paved Trail
△1	Route Starting Point
3-7	Route Number
∿	This Route
⊙	Direction of Travel
✶	Named Point
▣	Viewpoint
⌒	Gate
!	Use Caution
🚶	Hiking Route
∿∿	Streams, Rivers
▱	Lakes
⫰	Wetlands
▬	Mud Flats
▬	Water
▭	Parks
▢	Military Boundary (restricted use)
P	Parking
▣	Facility
══	Highway
══	Primary Road
──	Other Road
┼┼┼	Railroad

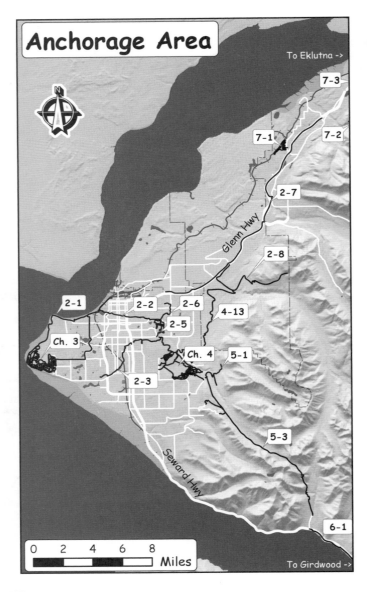

Anchorage Area

To Eklutna ->

To Girdwood ->

0 2 4 6 8 Miles

Chapter 1
Before You Ride

Bicycling in Anchorage

One of the best things about being a mountain biker living in Alaska's largest city is the easy access to miles of trails. By way of a network of dirt routes and paved greenbelt trails, one can bike more than a dozen miles from the largest park on the east side of the city to the west side and the coast without riding on any streets.

The long days of the Alaska summer allow cyclists to take in evening rides without running out of daylight. Lighted trails and hard-packed snow trails allow riders to extend the season into the winter months. All this makes Anchorage a great mountain-biking city any time of the year.

The abundant trails offer opportunities for all levels of riders, with some easier routes leading to scenic views of mountains, lakes and even a glacier. All the routes covered in this guide are within the Municipality of Anchorage, which covers 1,956 square miles from Portage to Eklutna and includes part of Chugach State Park. The trails may lead you to a berry patch or a burger joint, to a playground or a waterfall. They will also lead you closer to the wildlife that lives in and near the city. These are the things that make riding here memorable—it's not just the trails, but where they take you.

Bears

All of Anchorage is bear territory and in recent years the animals have been spotted as far west as popular Kincaid Park. Yet an outdoor enthusiast can go years without spotting either the more common black bear or a grizzly (brown) bear. Before venturing onto the trails, get familiar with bear behavior and how you should behave in bear territory. Bear safety classes are available through local outdoor shops and government agencies. Several publications on the subject are available at bookstores and outdoors-oriented shops. Most helpful and easy to use are agency websites, some of which are listed in the Resources section of this book.

Pay close attention to the trailhead signs that announce recent bear encounters and the date of the encounter. Not every sighting is listed, but the signs give details about the nature of the encounter and its location.

Moose

As important as bear safety is moose safety. Not as much has been written about this topic, but these ungulates can be as deadly to humans as bears. Approximately 200 to 300 moose make Anchorage their year-round home, and it is common to see them in parks and on greenbelt trails. You may see them crossing roads or wandering through neighborhoods and even downtown, especially in winter. Their numbers in urban areas may triple in winter as they leave the mountains in search of food. Always yield the trail to moose, which can weigh as much as 1,500 pounds. This may require you to either take a detour through overgrown brush or foot-deep snow to continue on your ride, or to backtrack. But an upset moose will charge even under what seems like no provocation. Be careful to not get between a cow moose and her calves.

Plants

Alaska has some plants to avoid when riding the area trails. Among them are two troublesome examples: devil's club and cow parsnip, sometimes called "pootchski."

Devil's club is a towering plant with broad, sprawling leaves that can grow up to 8 feet tall. The stems and branches are covered with sharp thorns. Even the young shoots can scratch the flesh. A similar-looking plant, cow parsnip, is more insidious because its effects aren't immediately evident.

Cow parsnip also grows up to 8 feet tall. It has broad leaves and a large white composite flower atop its hollow stalk. For some people, contact with the plant causes increased sensitivity to the sun, which can result in severe blisters that appear where you touched the plant. The blisters usually appear within a few days and can leave dark scars, which fade over time. There are few treatments, although some people insist that rinsing in cold water as soon as possible after touching the plant can prevent the blisters. It certainly can't hurt.

If you know you react to cow parsnip, avoid leaving your skin exposed on sunny days, especially when the plants are in bloom. Wear a lightweight long-sleeve shirt and pants or try to choose routes that won't be overgrown.

Water

Anchorage-area streams and lakes can contain giardia, which causes intestinal problems. Don't drink any water out of lakes or streams, no matter how clean they appear, without first running it through a filter or boiling the water for five minutes.

Trail Conditions

Dirt trails in municipal parks traditionally open on June 1 for the summer mountain biking season. On dry years, the trails can open earlier, but always check with municipal park officials before venturing out. If you ride when the trails are too wet, the ruts can remain on the trail all season. For early season riding, turn to the pavement to get your cycling legs in shape.

Paved greenbelt trails are a great option for most riders, but for serious training rides you're much better off on the road, on routes that have light traffic and either bike lanes or wide shoulders. If you plan to ride on greenbelt trails, place a bell on your bike and use it whenever approaching groups of people to alert them to your presence. Slow down and give them time to react. Be especially aware of small children, who may swerve unexpectedly, or dogs that may or may not be leashed.

During wet times of the year, some dirt trails have deep puddles of standing water. You should avoid riding around these puddles on singletrack trails because the practice widens the tread (trail surface), taking away from the character of the trail. If you don't want to ride through puddles, consider an alternate route until the trail dries.

Many of the routes listed in this book are ski, mushing or skijor (a skier pulled by one or two dogs) trails during the snow season, which typically runs from November through March. It's important that in the winter cyclists stay off trails that are designated for skis only or for mushing. You should stay on multi-use trails, and even skijor trails, and yield to other users. Some rare icy or snowless winters open up opportunities to bike on trails that are normally off limits, such as the mushing and ski trails. Check with the Nordic Skiing Association, park officials and bike shops to learn the trail conditions. Chapter Eight has more information on winter bicycling.

Trail Names

Trails in the Anchorage area are often named for trail pioneers, Alaska animals, or the topography that the route covers. What's important about the trail name? For many people, a name makes the route easier to remember or describe to others. Some trails in this guide are named with numbers only, such as "5 Km Loop." Other trails have more than one name. For example, many locals refer to the Tour of Anchorage Trail, but this is actually a route made up of several successive trails, each with its own name. Still other trails, mostly singletracks, have no names at all. Mountain bikers have given names to some routes, but you won't find those names on any maps.

A few trails in this guide have no official names, but they may have nicknames. Where this occurs, it will be noted that it is a commonly used name or a name used to avoid the confusion of referring to the routes as "Unnamed Trail 1" or "Unnamed Trail 2." Perhaps this will make it easier to follow the guide and remember the trails. Maybe the names will catch on.

Distance

Depending on how accurately a bike computer is calibrated, you may get mileage readings different from those used here. Distances in this guide are rounded to the nearest tenth of a mile unless otherwise noted.

Ride Ratings

What makes a trail more or less difficult depends on the rider. Distance can be a factor, especially early in the season. Steepness of climbs and descents can make a route more difficult for those not used to the terrain. The surface, such as the rocks and roots of some singletracks, is also a factor.

These rides are rated for the average mountain biker who gets out once a week. The intent is to give riders an idea of what to expect and to determine whether a route is right for them. New riders may want to use this guide to set goals. A ride ratings chart in the appendix will help you choose a route. Most of all, have fun!

Recommended Equipment

All of the rides in this book can be done with a standard mountain bike. On some routes, such as those that are paved, you may choose to ride a road bike or a hybrid. On some dirt trails, a rider with no suspension might wish for the extra control offered by a full-suspension bike. Others may like the challenge of riding a cyclocross or "cross bike" on some of the moderate dirt trails. Whatever bicycle type you choose, make sure that it is in good condition, with the tires properly inflated for the terrain and the chain lubricated. Make sure that the bike fits you. If you have any question on fit or the condition of your bicycle, you should take it to your favorite shop to consult with a professional.

These days, there's no reason to suffer an ill-fitting bike seat. Models for men and women are available at local shops and will make your riding experience more enjoyable so you'll want to bike more rather than dreading the next ride.

Following is a checklist for necessary equipment. This list is designed for those who want to be prepared for most situations while riding in the woods. Remember, it's always better to carry more than you need and be self-sufficient even when riding with friends on local trails.

Checklist

- **Helmet:** Get one that fits you comfortably and doesn't shift around as you ride.

- **Gloves:** Protect your hands in a crash or from blisters caused by the handlebar.

- **Padded cycling shorts:** Comfortable; they keep you from getting sore while in the saddle. Wear them as your base layer, with nothing underneath. Styles vary and include tight lycra; baggy shorts with a liner; a padded liner that can be worn under other shorts or tights; or skorts, a skirt with a built-in lycra short.

- **Sunglasses or sport shields:** Not just to protect your eyes from the sun, but also from low hanging branches, bugs and flying debris.

- **Hydration:** Carry a water bottle or a hydration backpack or fanny pack. It will help you stay hydrated so you can ride longer. Hydration packs often have storage space for tools and other necessities.

- **Tire pump:** In case you need to change your tire pressure or repair a flat. Know how your pump works!

  Keep your tools in a seat bag. That way the kit is a part of the bike and you'll always have your tools with you. Your seat bag tool kit should include:

- **Tire levers:** To remove the tire.

- **Spare tube:** It's quicker to replace than to patch (think rainy days, mosquitoes, etc.).

- **Patch kit:** In case you get another flat.

- **Chain tool:** If you break your chain, you want to know how to use this tool.

- **Chain link:** or pin To reconnect the chain if necessary.

- **Metric hex set:** At least sizes 4, 5 and 6 mm Allen wrenches to tighten or adjust almost anything on your bike.

- **Small screwdriver:** To adjust brakes.

- **Duct tape:** Wrap some around the body of your pump to use for emergency repairs.

- **Rag or old sock:** Bundle your toolkit in a sock or rag before placing it in your seat bag. This keeps it from rattling around as you ride and keeps tools from rubbing a hole in your spare tube.

Other useful items to carry include:

- **Swiss army knife:** For derailleur repairs and opening bottles.

- **Shock pump:** If you have air shocks on your bike, you may decide to carry the pump with you for adjustments, especially if you're still getting used to the ride of the bike.

- **Fenders:** They keep the mud out of your eyes and the stripe off your back. The newer lightweight fenders attach easily.

- **Jacket:** A lightweight wind jacket can keep you warm if the weather changes or if you are making a long descent. Carry it just in case of an emergency even on summer days.

- **Food:** Even if you ate just before you started the ride, take some food with you in case you bonk (suddenly lose all your energy) or end up staying out longer than you expected. Good to share with friends if they didn't fuel up!

- **Chain lubricant:** Don't be one of the squeaky ones. Longer rides or wet conditions may require this item for smooth-shifting and a silent chain.

- **Money:** For food or drinks during long rides in the city.

- **Cell phone:** Can get you out of trouble in an emergency, but don't rely on it unless you know it will work from where you are. Even Anchorage has pockets where there's limited coverage, including some parts of Kincaid Park.

- **Quarter:** To make a local call (for those with no cell phone) in case of a breakdown.

- **Flashing tail light:** In case you get caught in the dark at the end of a ride and must take a road home.

- **This book!**

- **Cycling computer:** Ride distances are provided in this book, and with a computer you will know where and when to turn.

- **Trail map:** Especially if you're riding in an area for the first time.

- **Bug dope:** If you ride with a group, you're more likely to want insect repellent since you will stop more often. If you prefer to not use the bug dope, a lightweight long-sleeve top will keep the mosquitoes at bay.

- **Identification:** An emergency contact name and phone number are helpful in case you crash or have some sort of emergency, especially when riding alone or with a group of people who are new to you. Carry a health insurance card if you have one.

- **First aid kit:** Bandages of various sizes, ointment and pain relievers.

- **Good old-fashioned common sense:** The list above is not exhaustive, but a little common sense takes up no room at all. Even on a day trip, make someone aware of where you're going and when you expect to return.

- **Winter equipment:** See Chapter Eight, on winter bicycling.

Trailhead Safety

Here are some words of warning to cyclists parking at area trailheads, no matter the time of year or day or area of town. Trailheads have become targets for "smash and grab" thieves. They wait until no one is around, then break windows to steal valuables from cars. Purses, wallets, cameras, passports, checks and credit cards are among the items stolen every year. To protect yourself, note any suspicious behavior, such as people hanging out at trailheads who aren't dressed for park activities or those who drive into then out of the lot. Trust your instincts. Don't leave your wallet or other valuable items in your car while you're using the parks. Either take them with you in a pack or leave them at home.

If you must leave a duffel of items in the car and you don't have a trunk, empty the contents of the bag into the open so that thieves can see you have nothing of interest. The best prevention to trailhead theft is to leave everything at home except what you can take on the ride.

Getting Here – For Visitors Flying to Anchorage

Several airlines offer flights to Anchorage, with nonstop routes available from cities such as Seattle, Salt Lake City, Denver and Minneapolis. Check with your airline on the cost of bringing your bicycle with you. Standard cardboard bike boxes and plastic bike cases are considered oversized luggage. Fees for checking a bike can range from $50 to $80 each way, depending on the airline. Shipping from the Lower 48 by package carrier, such as UPS or FedEx, will typically cost over $100. However, the return shipment may be considerably less. If you plan several days of biking, it will be worthwhile to bring your own bike for a couple of reasons: there are not many mountain bikes available to rent in the Anchorage area, and, unless you reserve ahead of time, you may not be able to find a bike to fit you or your riding style.

Many cyclists prefer to ride their own bike whenever possible. Especially when riding on unfamiliar trails, they will know how the bike is going to respond and how the shifters work! If you do wish to rent a bike, see Resources to find out where to rent one.

You can purchase a hard case for your bike or use a cardboard box from a bike shop near your home. Some shops may charge a small fee for the box, but it is usually for the service they provide in saving the best boxes and some of the packaging material as well as answering a few questions on how to box it. They will also box your bike for a small fee. Prices for hard cases start at about $300. If you use a hard case, be sure you have a place to store it while visiting. Area shops may charge a small storage fee if they have space available. Baggage storage is available at the airport for $5 to $7 per day. No weekly rates are available.

Pack additional items in your bike box to help protect the bike. (After all, you're paying the airline to ship an oversized box, so you might as well get your money's worth.) Use your sleeping bag and pad, riding shoes, tent, hydration pack, whatever fits. Don't pack your helmet in your box. Instead, take it in your carry-on so you know it isn't getting damaged. Remember to leave plenty of time to check in at the airport in case you're chosen for a baggage search.

Once in Anchorage, you will find several locally owned shops, all specializing in different lines of bikes. They can reassemble your bike for reasonable rates. And you will usually leave with some tips on which trails to hit first as well as where to find the best food and brew in town. Many hotels offer courtesy shuttle services. Check with your hotel to see if they will have room for your bike box in the shuttle. Some Anchorage taxis can also accommodate a bike box, so you can take the bike directly to a shop for reassembly.

If you want to hook up with local riders, two clubs are active in the Anchorage area. The Arctic Bicycle Club (ABC) sponsors road and mountain racing and offers recreational rides. The local chapter of the Women's Mountain Bike & Tea Society (WOMBATS), has been active in Anchorage since 2000. They offer recreational rides and clinics for women of all abilities. Weekend rides are often listed as "coed." See the Resources section for club contacts.

The Lay of the Land

For those new to the Anchorage area, the long summer daylight hours and the position of the sun during different times of the year can make it difficult to know which way is north. Magnetic north varies considerably from true north. The more level west side of Anchorage juts into Cook Inlet, so that water borders the city to the north, west and south. Moving inland, the terrain becomes more hilly, then mountainous with the Chugach Mountains bordering much of the city to the east.

If you remember this, on a clear day from a high point you will be able to find your way through the city. If the clouds drop and you're on the flats, get to the nearest trail marker to reorient yourself before continuing.

Rules of the Trail

These rules are provided with permission from the International Mountain Bicycling Association (IMBA). See Chapter Eight for specific winter cycling rules.

When riding on the trails in Alaska, or anywhere in the world, remember IMBA's "Rules of the Trail."

The way we ride today shapes mountain bike trail access tomorrow. Do your part to preserve and enhance our sport's access and image by observing the following rules of the trail, formulated by IMBA. These rules are recognized around the world as the standard code of conduct for mountain bikers. IMBA's mission is to promote mountain bicycling that is environmentally sound and socially responsible.

1. Ride on open trails only.

Respect trail and road closures (ask if uncertain); avoid

trespassing on private land; obtain permits or other authorization as may be required. Federal and state wilderness areas are closed to cycling. The way you ride will influence trail management decisions and policies.

2. Leave no trace.

Be sensitive to the dirt beneath you. Recognize different types of soils and trail construction; practice low-impact cycling. Wet and muddy trails are more vulnerable to damage. When the trail bed is soft, consider other riding options. This also means staying on existing trails and not creating new ones. Don't cut switchbacks. Be sure to pack out at least as much as you pack in.

3. Control your bicycle!

Inattention for even a second can cause problems. Obey all bicycle speed regulations and recommendations.

4. Always yield trail.

Let your fellow trail users know you're coming. A friendly greeting or bell is considerate and works well; don't startle others. Show your respect when passing by slowing to a walking pace or even stopping. Anticipate other trail users around corners or in blind spots. Yielding means slow down, establish communication, be prepared to stop if necessary and pass safely.

5. Never scare animals.

All animals are startled by an unannounced approach, a sudden movement or a loud noise. This can be dangerous for you, others and the animals. Give animals extra room and time to adjust to you. When passing horses use special care and follow directions from the horseback riders (ask if uncertain). Running cattle and disturbing wildlife is a serious offense. Leave gates as you found them, or as marked.

6. Plan ahead.

Know your equipment, your ability and the area in which you are riding—and prepare accordingly. Be self-sufficient at all times, keep your equipment in good repair and carry necessary supplies for changes in weather or other conditions. A well-executed trip is a satisfaction to you and not a burden to others. Always wear a helmet and appropriate safety gear.

Chapter 2

Early Season & Paved Trail Riding

While waiting for the dirt trails to open, you can head out onto the paved roads and bike paths to build your miles so you're ready for the challenges of off-road riding. A favorite early season ride is the Glenn Highway Trail, a separated path that runs along the highway from Anchorage to Chugiak. It's relatively flat and typically will be one of the first trails to be clear of snow. Traffic on the highway is usually busy, so you may want to avoid the morning or evening commute times on your recreational forays. Anchorage also has a growing network of greenbelt trails.

Greenbelt Routes

The three main greenbelt routes in the Anchorage Bowl are the Campbell Creek Trail, the Lanie Fleischer Chester Creek Trail and the Tony Knowles Coastal Trail. The first two connect neighborhoods and parks to one another and offer year-round recreation for residents right from their doorsteps. The north end of the Coastal Trail does the same, but once it reaches Earthquake Park on the west side of Anchorage, it's far from any more neighborhoods.

Each trail has numerous access points. The descriptions here will cover each route from one end to the other and note some major access points, those for which vehicle parking is available.

These greenbelts occasionally intersect roadways. Use caution and heed the warning signs when you approach the intersections.

Plans have been in the works for a number of years to extend the Coastal Trail farther south to Potter Marsh, but the extension is probably years away from being built. The municipality also plans to connect two segments of the

Campbell Creek Trail by building a tunnel under the Seward Highway. When complete, it will provide a much-needed safe route under this major road. A paved route is also planned for the university area and would connect the Chester Creek and Campbell Creek trails. Another trail in the works is the Ship Creek Trail, just north of downtown.

Each of these projects will result in more options for cyclists making their way through Anchorage.

2-1 Tony Knowles Coastal Trail

Difficulty: Easy to moderate due to the longer distance and some hills. The loop option has some road riding.

Surface: Paved.

Winter: Yes.

Distance: 20.6-mile round trip; 20.2-mile loop.

A former Alaska governor, Tony Knowles, was mayor of Anchorage from 1981 to 1987 and served on the municipal assembly during the 1970s.

The Coastal Trail is the gem of Anchorage's paved trail system. From its start at Second Avenue downtown to its current terminus at the Kincaid Park Chalet, the trail's 10-plus miles offer views of the city, the Chugach Mountains, Denali (Mt. McKinley), Mt. Susitna (Sleeping Lady) and Fire Island. It passes railroad tracks, several parks and the airport before it takes you away from the crowds to the relative quiet of a rural path. Most of the trail has a moderate grade, but the final climb can be a challenge to newer riders, especially early in the season.

A proposal to extend the trail south to Potter Marsh,

just beyond Rabbit Creek Road in South Anchorage, has been controversial but would double the length of the trail. While many Anchorage residents support the extension along the coast, some living along the route are concerned about loss of property and privacy issues. Some residents worry about the effect a shoreline route would have on wildlife in the Anchorage Coastal Wildlife Refuge. Funding is also a concern in a time of tight federal and state budgets.

The Coastal Trail links downtown to many neighborhoods and to other trails, creating great commuting opportunities on bike, foot or skis. On any day or evening, you will see dozens (maybe hundreds in the summer) of other trail users, mostly in the first few miles from downtown to Earthquake Park. An increasing number of families and visitors use the trail for fitness and to enjoy the scenery, so be aware of the possible large number of trail users but don't let it discourage you from taking in this ride.

Because the Coastal Trail is so well used, watch your speed and use caution when approaching groups of people. To avoid collisions, pay attention to the center lines on the trails.

The northern end of the trail is at the intersection of 2nd Avenue and H Street, downtown. More people begin at Elderberry Park, at 5th and N, or at Westchester Lagoon. The mileposts start at Westchester Lagoon, where the Coastal Trail intersects the Lanie Fleischer Chester Creek Trail. This description follows the trail from the 2nd Street entrance. If you're riding to the trailhead, be aware that it is illegal to ride on the sidewalks in a business district, so stay on the street and follow the rules of the road to arrive at the trailhead.

Getting to the Trailhead

From the intersection of 5th Avenue and H Street downtown, go north. At 3rd Avenue, H becomes Christensen Drive. Take Christensen down the hill (a white building housing the Snow Goose Restaurant & Brewery is on the right) and turn left at the next intersection, 2nd Avenue. The trailhead is just ahead.

Alternative Trailheads

Elderberry Park: To begin riding at Elderberry Park, take 5th Avenue west from downtown toward Cook Inlet and cross L Street. Go down the hill; parking is on the right.

Westchester Lagoon: To reach Westchester Lagoon from downtown, drive south on L Street (which becomes Minnesota Drive). Turn right (west) onto 15th Avenue. The first parking lot is on the left. A second parking lot is available just past the intersection of 15th and U Street.

If you're driving from the south, go north on Minnesota. Turn left (west) at 13th Street (15th doesn't go through), then right onto Inlet Place. Go left on 12th, then left on N Street to go around Inlet View Elementary School. Turn right on 15th to arrive at the lagoon.

Mi. 0.0 From 2nd Avenue and H Street, cross a wooden bridge, heading for the coast. The busy Port of Anchorage and the Alaska Railroad are to the right.

Mi. 0.3 Elderberry Park is to the left, as is the historic Oscar Anderson House. Play equipment and restrooms are available at the park. Keep to the right side of the trail as you descend and ride through a tunnel, one of several that pass under the Alaska Railroad tracks.

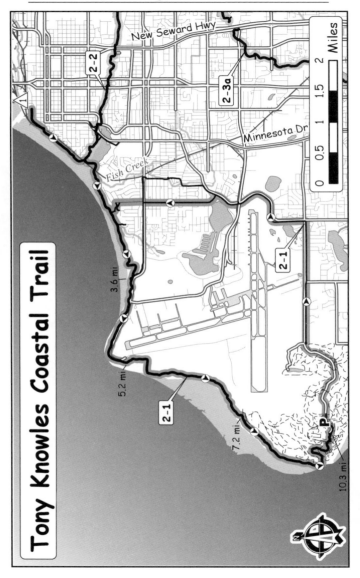

After leaving the tunnel, you'll arrive at a small park named Hannah Cove. Point McKenzie is across the water. When the tide is out, notice the clay-like soil along the coast. These are the mud flats, which look inviting but can be deadly because of the fluid properties of the soils. Don't enter the mud flats!

Mi. 0.6   At the top of a knoll are a pair of benches for enjoying the view. Another rise takes you into some trees and a more sheltered area before you descend again.

Mi. 1.1   Pass a bench and the Chester Creek Sewage Pump Station, on the left before riding through a second railroad tunnel.

Mi. 1.2   Cross a wooden bridge and turn right to remain on the Coastal Trail. (To the left is the Chester Creek Trail.) The route makes its way between Westchester Lagoon on your left and the railroad on your right. On a clear day, you may want to pull over to the side of the trail to enjoy the view of the Chugach Mountains.

Mi. 1.5   Cross a boardwalk over a marshy area. (There's another trailhead here with about four parking spaces.) Pass through the third railroad tunnel. After the tunnel, the trail winds along the coast toward Fish Creek. A wall to the left side of the trail and a fence to the right make this part of the trail narrow. Keep to the right side of the trail and slow down.

Mi. 1.7   Cross Fish Creek. A few benches offer a place to sit and look out over the water.

Mi. 2.4   After a short hill, arrive at Lyn Ary Park, which features an overlook, ball fields, and, up the hill to the left, a playground. To stay on the Coastal Trail, pedal straight ahead. (Left takes you to Turnagain Parkway and Northern Lights Boulevard.) The trail takes you westward near the water, then curves inland and climbs. The terrain off the side of the trail resembles moguls, one result of the 1964 Good Friday earthquake, which destroyed the homes in this part of the city.

Mi. 3.6 A four-way intersection is at the top of the hill. Straight ahead is the Coastal Trail. To the left is the parking area for Earthquake Park; to the right there are benches and an interpretive display about the '64 quake that gave this park its name.

Mi. 4.1 Cross a driveway for a large gravel parking area just off Northern Lights Boulevard. This is a popular place for people to look at the mountains of the Alaska Range and the city skyline.

Mi. 4.8 Arrive at a small pullout with a bench at the top of a hill. The next stretch of trail narrows and can have obstructed views. Keep to the right and watch your speed as you descend. The trail makes an abrupt left at the bottom of the hill, then climbs briefly. Don't be alarmed by low jets taking off and landing at Ted Stevens Anchorage International Airport.

Mi. 5.2 Arrive at the driveway to the parking lot at Point Woronzof. This popular parking area offers views to the west and access to a rocky beach below.

Mi. 5.3 Cross a driveway for the water treatment facility. This is the final parking area before you reach the Kincaid Chalet in about five miles. You'll pass several pullouts featuring benches that offer views over the inlet.

Mi. 7.2 Ride past the Anchorage Regional Compost Facility on the left.

Mi. 7.8 Cross a wooden bridge that spans a small gorge. Here you'll have a choice to stay on the paved route or turn left to enter the Sisson Loop dirt trail (mile 1.6 of Route 3-10). To reach the chalet, continue on the pavement.

Mi. 8.4 Emerge from the trees into an open area above some ponds. The Sisson Loop is beyond the ponds. Ride past more pullouts and two more entrances to the Sisson Loop.

Mi. 9.3 Pass the final pullout on the right before the trail cuts inland and begins to clin_____ ___ ___ ___ _____ pull-out, where the trail curves left, a _____ right to the beach below.) Pace you_____ gears to make a steady climb to t_____

Mi. 10.3 The trail forks. Stay to the right to ride a loop route back to Lyn Ary Park and on to downtown, or go left to the chalet. The chalet offers restrooms, an information counter and snack machines.

You can turn around here to ride the Coastal Trail back to downtown, or ride the loop option, which includes some road riding, bike path sections and a few stretches where you can choose to take either the road or the path.

Loop Option

From mile 10.3 of the Coastal Trail, continue straight and ride the bike path east (toward the Chugach Mountains).

Mi. 10.7 The bike path ends. Enter the roadway.

Mi. 11.7 Pass the Raspberry Road parking lot on the left.

Mi. 12.1 Exit Kincaid Park and ride either on the bike path on the south side of the road or on the right shoulder of the road.

Mi. 14.0 Approach the intersection of Jewel Lake and Raspberry roads. Because this is a busy intersection, the safest way to cross Raspberry is to take the bike path to the stoplight. If you're on the road, veer onto the path when you reach Fountain Street.

Mi. 14.1 Cross Raspberry at the light and ride north on the path on the west side of Jewel Lake Road. (There's a Tastee Freez on the west end of the shopping center, plus a fine dining restaurant, the Kincaid Grill, on the east end.) Use caution when approaching the next few intersections because drivers often pull into the crosswalks. Stop signs for cyclists are placed at some of the intersections, so drivers expect you to stop!

Mi. 14.6 Continue straight as a trail to the right goes under the road.

Mi. 15.0 The airport is to the left on the other side of a chain-link fence.

Mi. 15.3 Across the road to the right is Connors Lake, which is popular with dog owners. It has an off-leash area and a network of skijoring trails. The park is also home to nesting Pacific loons. Continue straight across Old International Airport Road.

Mi. 15.5 Cross International Airport Road and ride over the railroad tracks. You're now on Spenard Road. Ride the sidewalk a short distance, past the float planes and hotels. At the stoplight, turn left on Wisconsin. (If you want to ride the bike lane, cross Wisconsin, then go left on the sidewalk until the bike lane begins.) This route follows the bike path running alongside Wisconsin.

Mi. 16.8 Arrive at Balto Seppala Park, which has picnic tables, some play equipment and a soccer field. Continue north.

Mi. 17.0 Just after 31st Street, cross Northern Lights Boulevard. The street is now called Turnagain Parkway. Cross Turnagain Parkway to ride with traffic on the east side of the street.

Mi. 17.5 After a stop sign, Lyn Ary Park appears on the left (northwest) corner. Stay on Turnagain until you arrive at a trailhead marker on the left side of the street.

Mi. 17.6 Enter the trail and ride down the hill, past the ball fields, to arrive at a "T" intersection with the Coastal Trail.

Mi. 17.8 Turn right at the "T" to return to your downtown starting point, almost 2.4 miles away.

Mi. 20.2 Arrive back at 2nd and H.

2-2   Lanie Fleischer Chester Creek Trail

Difficulty: Easy; narrow tunnels can have ice in winter and spring.

Surface: Paved.

Winter: Yes.

Distance: 10.2 miles round trip.

Lanie Fleischer is a trail advocate who in the early 1970s envisioned a bike trail that would take riders from the mountains to the coast.

The Chester Creek Trail is a popular year-round route for commuters and trail users of all kinds. It links downtown to the universities and medical district and provides access to several parks. The parks are host to a number of activities from disc golf and bike polo to soccer and basketball. The almost limitless range of activities you may witness on a given day as you pass by on the trail is testament to Anchorage's love of getting into the outdoors, where people of diverse backgrounds and interests share an appreciation of the parks.

The trail is just over five miles long and runs east from Westchester Lagoon, passing through several tunnels and over bridges that cross Chester Creek as it meanders toward the inlet. The greenbelt route ends where it becomes a street-side path at the intersection of Northern Lights Boulevard and Wesleyan Drive.

While the tunnels let riders avoid the busy roads, be aware that ice in some tunnels during the winter and spring can make them bumpy and slippery to ride through.

This route begins at the intersection of the Chester Creek Trail and Tony Knowles Coastal Trail in Margaret Eagan Sullivan Park. The route has mile markers, and the mileage descriptions for this ride correspond with them. Start at an iron worker's memorial just east of mile 1.2 of the Coastal Trail, next to a pair of benches. See "Alternative Trailheads" in Route 2-1 for directions to Westchester Lagoon.

Mi. 0.0 Ride east toward the mountains, past play equipment and two parking lots, the second of which is the parking lot for ice skating on the lagoon and provides

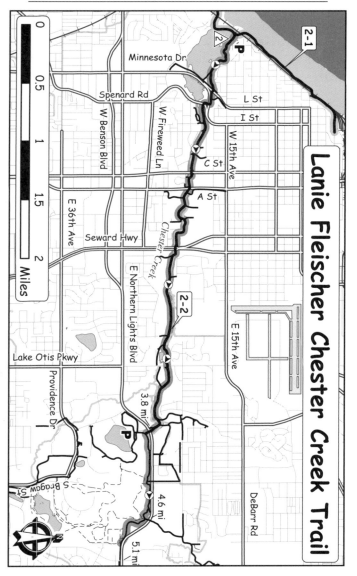

Lanie Fleischer Chester Creek Trail

access to a small dock. After the second parking lot, stay on the paved path as it bends away from the lagoon. (A dirt-path shortcut has become popular, but the mileage for this ride stays on the pavement.) Veer back toward the lagoon, then ride along side the water.

Mi. 0.4   Go left at the first intersection. You'll pass a disc golf course during this part of the ride. (Or, if you continue straight ahead and turn right at the next junction, you'll climb West High Hill and arrive at Hillcrest Drive, across from the school.)

Mi. 0.5   Go left, then turn right almost immediately to ride under southbound Minnesota Drive, the first of several tunnels.

Mi. 0.7   Slow down before the route makes a sharp right to enter the tunnel under northbound Minnesota. It then curves left, to enter a third tunnel, this one under Spenard Road.

Mi. 0.9   Stay straight as you pass a neighborhood entrance, then ride past a stairway on the left.

Mi. 1.0   Ride through the tunnel under Arctic Boulevard and arrive at Valley of the Moon Park, known to many as Rocket Ship Park for its original playground equipment, now replaced by a new spacecraft-like structure. The park also has a picnic shelter and restrooms. Ball fields are just east of the restrooms.

Mi. 1.2   Continue straight. (To the right, a bridge crosses Chester Creek to a neighborhood. To the left, you can enter the ball fields.)

Mi. 1.3   Ride past an arched bridge (which crosses the creek and leads to community gardens) and under C

Street. Veer right to cross a bridge and arrive at an area informally referred to as Gorilla Park, named for the statues on the west side of the grounds. You may see cyclists playing bike polo here on summer weeknights. Veer left after leaving the bridge.

Mi. 1.5 Ride toward the next underpass (A Street). The trail is very close to the creek and slopes down toward it. Use caution in the winter and spring when the trail may be icy. Continue straight. (A left turn after the underpass takes you to Sullivan Arena, Mulcahy Stadium and a skate park.)

Mi. 1.6 Continue straight. (Going to the right takes you uphill toward Fireweed Lane.) Stay straight at the next intersection as well. (Turning left and crossing a bridge will take you to the sports complex. For a little singletrack trail, go left, then before the bridge turn right and follow the dirt trail next to the creek. The trail rejoins the paved route at a bridge just past mile 1.8.)

Mi. 1.8 Veer left toward the bridge. (Note the single-track on both sides of the trail as you approach the bridge.) Cross the bridge and veer right to remain on the route.

Mi. 2.1 Pass through a tunnel under the Seward Highway. Veer right and cross a bridge to arrive at Woodside Park, then veer left. (If you go straight, you'll climb a hill into the woods and emerge at a neighborhood at the east end of Fireweed Lane.) Pass a soccer field to the right as you continue.

Mi. 2.4 Enter the woods and continue following the creek. (A trail to the left crosses a bridge into a neighborhood and leads to Karluk Street.)

Tip

Warm spells during the winter and low nighttime temperatures in the spring cause parts of the trail in this boggy area, from about mile 2.5 to 2.7, to be covered by frozen overflow. The bumpy ice often cascades over the trail. Use care when riding here. Studded tires help, but lowering your tire pressure will also give you extra traction.

Mi. 2.9   Stay straight. (A trail to the right leads to Lake Otis Parkway.)

Mi. 3.0   Just after the three-mile mark, you'll arrive at a pond. A small pullout has a picnic table, bench and bike rack. You can usually see ducks on the pond all summer. Veer left to cross the culverted creek.

Mi. 3.1   Ride through the tunnel under Lake Otis Parkway and continue straight, past the ball fields and play equipment at Tikishla Park.

Option

Mi. 3.2   Across from the ball fields, you may notice a dirt trail to the left. It takes you through the woods and arrives at a "T." Turn right at the "T" to return to the paved trail, reentering at mile 3.5.

Mi. 3.6   Turn right and cross a wooden bridge. After the bridge, take another right and climb.

Mi. 3.8   Cross the bridge over Northern Lights Boulevard. (Just after the bridge, you may notice a dirt trail veering right that connects with the paved trail. If you're riding fast, the berm is a jump, so use caution on this little shortcut.)

After the bridge, you'll arrive at a "T." Veer left to continue on this route. (Go right to arrive at Goose Lake and make your way to the U-Med District, where you'll find the campuses of the University of Alaska Anchorage (UAA) and Alaska Pacific University (APU), Providence Alaska Medical Center and, closer to Tudor Road, the Alaska Native Medical Center and other health offices.

Mi. 4.0 Veer right and begin a gradual climb. (Straight would take you to Northern Lights and a bus stop.)

Mi. 4.3 Veer left toward Northern Lights then follow the route as the trail curves right. Across the street is East High School. Ride past another bus stop. (If you turn right onto the dirt trails, you will arrive at the Mahaffey Trails on the campuses of UAA and APU.)

Mi. 4.6 Continue straight. (To the right is an entrance to the dirt-surface Mahaffey Trails, Route 2-5. Going to the left and across a bridge will take you to Russian Jack Springs Park, Route 2-6.)

Mi. 4.9 Cross a utility access road and continue straight. (Turn right to ride a power line route that will take you to University Lake and on to Tudor Road, Route 2-4.)

Mi. 5.0 Continue straight and descend on the path as it transitions from a greenbelt trail to a street-side path.

Mi. 5.1 Intersect with Wesleyan Drive at the stoplight. A street-side path parallels Northern Lights to Patterson Street, just before Muldoon Road.

2-3a Campbell Creek Trail – West of Seward Highway

Difficulty: Easy.

Surface: Paved.

Winter: Yes.

Distance: 8.6 miles round trip.

The Campbell Creek Trail is very much a neighborhood route. On a summer day, families and kids fish or play in the creek. Neighbors walk dogs; families spend an afternoon at Taku Lake. The route has over a dozen neighborhood access points, making recreation easily accessible to everyone along the trail.

The trail runs from the intersection of Dimond Boulevard and Northwood Drive, northeast toward the intersection of International Airport Road and the southbound frontage road of the Seward Highway. There is one road crossing, at Potter Drive.

The Anchorage Areawide Trails Plan calls for the trail to be extended under the Seward Highway so it can connect to a newly built segment of the trail east of the highway and south of the busy Lake Otis and Tudor intersection. The connector will be a welcome addition to the trail system in this area where heavy vehicle traffic makes biking, particularly commuting, a perilous endeavor.

If you're driving to the trailhead, go west from the Minnesota and Dimond interchange. The Fred Meyer department store is on the left. The first stoplight after the store is Victor Road on the left and Northwood Street on the right. You can turn right here and park in this small

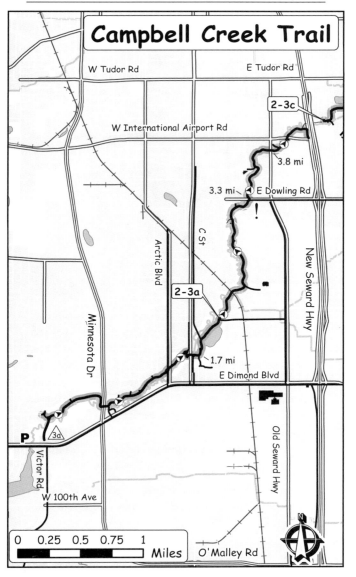

Campbell Creek Trail

pullout, where there's room for just a few cars, or continue west on Dimond, cross a bridge over Campbell Creek, and turn right into a parking lot. The sign tells you you're at the Campbell Creek Greenbelt. To get to the trailhead, ride the sidewalk back over the bridge to Northwood and turn left.

Mi. 0.0 Start the ride at the trailhead bollards and ride downhill.

Mi. 0.1 Stay right to ride the trail as you pass a few neighborhood entrances.

Mi. 0.7 Ride under Minnesota Drive.

Mi. 1.3 Stay left to ride under Arctic Boulevard.

Mi. 1.6 Go right and ride on a wood bridge over the creek. After the bridge, it seems that you are at a traffic circle on the bike path. Go left here and ride under C Street. Slow down to look at the artwork created for this portion of the trail. Silver fish leap upstream on the fence between the trail and the creek. The concrete abutment on the right is decorated with relief figures of a bear, beaver, moose and eagle—all animals you may encounter in the Anchorage area. As you emerge from under the bridge, three salmon-shaped chairs welcome you to rest under a light fixture designed to look like a fishing lure. It's a treat for trail users; you won't experience this public art from your car.

Mi. 1.7 The main trail stays left. The route to the right leads to a play area in Taku/Campbell Park. Besides playground equipment, there are tennis courts and a fitness station.

Mi 1.8 Ride alongside Taku Lake, on your right, and past a parking lot. In the next half mile, you'll ride over three more bridges as the creek meanders. You'll also pass under a railroad bridge.

Mi 2.4   Go left at this intersection.

Mi 3.0   Cross a private driveway, then a neighborhood trail entrance.

Mi 3.3   Caution! Arrive at a stop sign where the trail intersects Potter Drive. This is the only street crossing on the route, and signs tell you to dismount your bike before crossing. Cross a few more bridges and you'll see to the left, across the creek, the deck for the Arctic Roadrunner restaurant.

Mi 3.8   Ride under the Old Seward Highway. To the left you'll see the back deck of the Peanut Farm, another restaurant. Both are great choices if you want to have a meal out on the deck.

Mi 4.0   On the right side of the trail is the Sourdough Mining Company, another restaurant. Ride under International Airport Road.

Mi 4.2   Plans are in the works to connect the east and west sections of trail under the Seward Highway. The proposed route will turn left and cross the bridge here. (Some riders are crossing the bridge and following a singletrack dirt trail that leads under the present Seward Highway bridge over the Campbell Creek. The route has large boulders and little headroom, so it can be dangerous.) If you continue straight at mile 4.2, you will arrive at a point where the trail turns right to run parallel with the frontage road.

Mi 4.3   The trail ends at the intersection of the frontage road and International Airport Road.

2-3b Campbell Creek Trail – Lake Otis Parkway to Tudor Road

Difficulty: Easy.

Surface: Paved.

Winter: Yes.

Distance: 3 miles round trip.

This portion of the Campbell Creek Trail lets cyclists avoid the busy Lake Otis Parkway and Tudor Road intersection when riding between Lake Otis and the U-Med District. It also connects with the Tour of Anchorage route for those wanting to access Far North Bicentennial Park. This description begins at Campbell Creek Park, at the intersection of Lake Otis and 68th Avenue.

Mi. 0.0 From the locator map at Campbell Creek Park, ride straight, passing the castle like play area on your right, then veering right as a route joins from the left.

Mi. 0.1 Veer left as the route from the parking area enters from the right.

Mi. 0.3 Cross a large bridge over the meandering creek.

Mi. 0.4 Cross a second bridge. Just after the bridge, a right turn onto a viewing deck makes an interesting side trip, especially when salmon are in the creek. Continue east from the viewing deck.

Mi. 0.8 Just after arriving at a bench, you'll cross a pair of dog mushing tunnels. This is a great spot to watch sled dog races in the winter.

Mi. 0.9 A left turn takes you to the parking lot for the

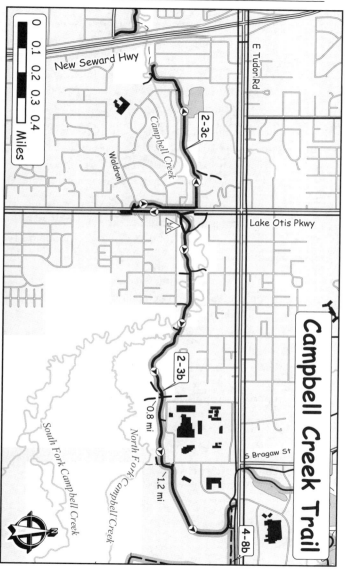

municipal Public Transportation Department. Where the trail empties into the parking lot, you can view a sculpture, by Richard S. Beyer, called Lunch Break. The artwork portrays a workman sitting on a rock having lunch and his surprise visitor. You may decide to take a break on a bench opposite the sculpture.

Return to the trail and turn left. You'll approach what is currently the end of Bragaw Street and a power line corridor. Construction to extend this street south is expected to begin in the summer of 2005. Stay right or watch for trail detours.

Mi. 1.2   Ride past the entrance to the Chuck Albrecht Sports Fields. Soon a view of the Chugach Mountains opens ahead of you.

Mi. 1.5   Arrive at a trail intersection with an informational sign on your left. From here, the Tour of Anchorage trail to the Hillside is the dirt trail to your right. If you go straight, you'll reach the Tudor Road street-side path, where you can go left to cross the road on the bridge and ride to the university area, or go right to take the path east, following Tudor Road. The path ends where Baxter Road and Campbell Airstrip Road intersect with Tudor.

2-3c   Campbell Creek Trail – Lake Otis Parkway to Seward Highway

Difficulty: Easy, with some street crossings and some street riding.

Surface: Paved.

Winter: Yes.

Distance: 2 miles round trip.

The eastern portion of the Campbell Creek Greenbelt trail allows you to navigate through the neighborhoods between Lake Otis Parkway and the New Seward Highway. In time, the route will be completed so that a paved trail connects under the highway to the western section of the trail, giving commuters and recreational riders a safe route that bypasses the busy interchange of the Seward Highway and Tudor Road. Some commuters walk their bikes along the creek under the Seward Highway. There's not much headroom for those using the dirt path and you must navigate among some large boulders, but the creekside route might be safer than riding along Tudor Road.

This route starts at the same spot as Route 2-3b, the intersection of Lake Otis and 68th Avenue, and travels in the opposite direction, west.

Mi. 0.0 Begin at the entrance to Campbell Creek Park and ride south on Lake Otis Parkway to Waldron Drive.

Mi. 0.1 Cross Lake Otis at the stoplight, then take the paved path as it veers away from the street for a short distance. Cross a narrow bridge. (An alternative goes south past a stairway and makes a hairpin left turn (0.2 mile) to ride down a ramp and through a tunnel. You would then cross Waldron at the Lake Otis stoplight and rejoin the route as it takes you north.)

Mi. 0.4 Turn left at 47th Court and ride the bike lane to the end of the block. Turn right onto the greenbelt trail and follow the route past Waldron Fields and Waldron Lake. The route passes a neighborhood entrance on the left, then curves left.

Mi. 1.0 The trail veers right as you ride past a bridge

on the left then continues west. The trail ends at the intersection of Pavalof Street and Rakof Avenue. Turn left onto Rakof to locate the dirt route under the highway.

Option

To stay on the neighborhood streets, ride west on Waldron Drive. Turn right onto Bartlett Drive, then right onto Cache Drive. Cache ends at a trailhead that goes to the Campbell Creek Trail. Turn left onto the paved route to reach the highway. Going straight on a dirt path will eventually lead to Tudor Road.

University Area and Russian Jack Springs Park

Two linked trail systems in the center of Anchorage provide riders with some surprises, including paved trails, dirt trails, and excellent commuting routes. The wooded areas with streams and small lakes provide a respite after the workday and are easily accessible from many neighborhoods. Because of the trails' proximity to homes, riders should always watch for walkers, runners, dogs and children. These parks can be busy on sunny days.

2-4 Connecting the Campbell Creek and Chester Creek Trails

Difficulty: Easy.

Surface: Wide dirt and gravel with some pavement.

Winter: Yes.

Distance: 3 miles round trip.

While there are several ways you can cross the university area, this route is the simplest and is considered multi-use for winter commuting. It also avoids the busiest part of the municipal park, an off-leash area for dogs.

Mi. 0.0   From the Tudor Road bridge, ride north and go through a tunnel under Ambassador Drive.

Mi. 0.3   Turn right at a "T" and follow a dirt path along the south side of University Lake.

Mi. 0.6   Cross a bridge and go straight. (Left goes to a soccer field.)

Mi. 0.8   Turn left just before the trail reaches another bridge. Follow the corridor north, passing between a neighborhood to your right and the university land on your left. (If you cross this second bridge, you will end up at a small park with play equipment.)

Mi. 1.5   Arrive at a gate across the access route. Go around the gate and just a few feet more to arrive at the Chester Creek Trail. Turn left to get to Russian Jack Springs or Westchester Lagoon. Turn right to ride east on a street-side path along Northern Lights Boulevard.

2-5   University Area—Mahaffey Trails

Difficulty: Moderate with some steep hills.

Surface: Mostly wide gravel and dirt.

Winter: No.

Distance: 3.8-mile loop.

With so many access points to the trails at Alaska Pacific University, it's sometimes tough to know where to begin. You can start near University Lake or Goose Lake or on the Chester Creek Trail. This description begins at mile 4.6 of the Chester Creek Trail, south of the bridge that leads to Russian Jack Springs Park.

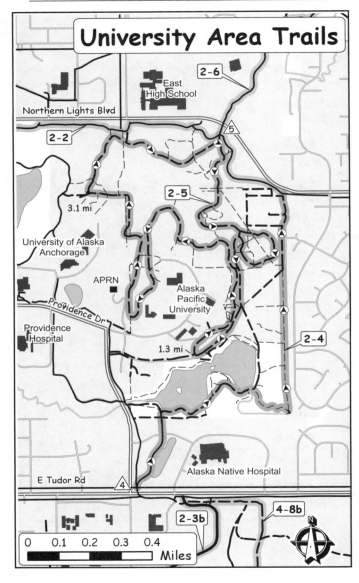

University Area Trails

2-6

East High School

Northern Lights Blvd

2-2

5

3.1 mi

2-5

University of Alaska Anchorage

APRN

Alaska Pacific University

Providence Dr

Providence Hospital

1.3 mi

2-4

E Tudor Rd

4

Alaska Native Hospital

2-3b

4-8b

| 0 | 0.1 | 0.2 | 0.3 | 0.4 |

Miles

N

Option

For those not biking to the trail, the most convenient parking area is at Goose Lake Park. From the Seward Highway, go east on Benson Boulevard. After LaTouche Street, Benson becomes Northern Lights Boulevard. Continue past Lake Otis Parkway. The next stoplight is UAA Drive, which is 1.4 miles east of the Seward Highway. Turn right, then take an immediate left to arrive at Goose Lake Park. The trail entrance is to the left, opposite the boathouse. You'll join the Chester Creek Trail at the 3.8-mile point and turn right to arrive at the beginning of this route.

APU posts trail closures during spring breakup, but the signs often go missing before the trails are dry. If no signs are present during the spring and the trails are still muddy, stay off them to prevent damage. A good rule of thumb is to wait until contiguous sections are dry. Expect to be allowed to use the trails by the end of May. Although a number of smaller social trails meander through the park, APU officials ask riders to stay on the main trails.

Mi. 0.0 Leave the pavement and enter the dirt trail into the woods. Turn left onto the main trail.

Mi. 0.2 Cross a power line access route and climb. Stay on the main route, passing a berm and trail to the left. You'll pass a number of singletracks, some of which are open to ride.

Mi. 0.4 Continue straight where you pass a power line to the left. Veer left at an intersection. (Right is a shortcut that lops off part of the loop.)

Mi. 0.5 Continue straight as a multi-use route crosses

the trail at an angle. The main trail loops around and you'll again cross this multi-use route at mile 0.7.

Mi. 0.8 Turn left. (Right is the end of the mile 0.4 shortcut.) Continue as the main trail climbs and descends.

Mi. 1.0 Go straight as a connector trail enters from the right.

Mi. 1.1 Emerge at the northwest corner of the soccer field. Go right and ride along the field.

Mi. 1.2 Leave the field and pass between a pair of metal posts.

Mi. 1.3 Arrive at a main multi-use trail and go right. Almost immediately, take another right onto the trails marked for ski only and begin a climb. Pass the first right turn (at mile 1.4), then descend on the second right and continue straight.

Mi. 1.7 Veer left when a connector trail enters from the right, then immediately turn right.

Mi. 1.9 Continue straight for a half mile or so as a number of routes enter from different directions, including a route to the right labeled "cut off." You'll make a longer climb, then the trail curves right and descends, approaching a parking lot.

Mi. 2.6 Veer right when you're opposite the Alaska Public Radio Network (APRN) building to stay on the main route.

Mi. 2.8 The trail curves left as the end of the "cut off" enters from the right and you descend to a boggy area. Just as you leave the woods, turn right onto a singletrack trail. The route curves left into a grassy area and veers right to approach a power line.

Mi. 2.9   Turn left at the power line. The trail becomes wider and climbs.

Mi. 3.1   At a four-way intersection, turn right. You may notice a "ski only" sign at the entrance.

Mi. 3.4   Continue straight as you cross an established gravel trail. (To the left are the Chester Creek Trail, Northern Lights Boulevard and East High School.)

Mi. 3.7   Watch for an unmarked trail and turn left to get to the Chester Creek Trail.

Mi. 3.8   End at the paved trail. Ride over the bridge to get to Russian Jack Springs Park.

2-6   Russian Jack Springs Park

Difficulty: Easy to moderate; more strenuous and technical for those on dirt routes.

Surface: Paved with options for dirt.

Winter: Yes, paved route only.

Distance: 4.4 miles round trip on pavement.

This park, according to the municipality's records, is named for Russian Jack Marchin, whose real name was Jacob Marunenko. A Russian immigrant, Marchin arrived in Anchorage in 1915. He is said to have lived in a cabin here with permission from the land's homesteaders, Peter Toloff and Nicholaus Dalopaulos. In 1937 Marchin killed a man, claiming he acted in self-defense, but he was convicted of manslaughter and served two and a half years in a federal penitentiary in Washington. Although he returned to Anchorage for a short time, he never lived in the cabin again.

Many riders, even mountain bikers, pass through Russian Jack Springs Park on their way to other trails, maybe even the dirt trails at APU or the Hillside. They may glance at the dirt trails as they speed by on the pavement, yet this 320-acre park on the east side of Anchorage offers a surprising number of dirt trails, including some fun singletrack.

When on your bicycle, you can access the park from several points, including the Chester Creek and APU trails, Boniface Parkway, and DeBarr Road. If you're driving, there is parking at the golf course off DeBarr or near the playing fields off Pine Street. But if you live within a few miles of the park, it's best to ride there. That's one of the beauties of Russian Jack Springs Park. It is in a central location for those on the east side of the city.

Most of the trails at Russian Jack are not paved. This description covers the paved route and some suggested dirt trails that are available after June 1. Other routes are left for riders to explore. The size of the park makes it difficult to truly get lost, at least for long. The route begins where it intersects with the Chester Creek Trail (Route 2-2). The paved route is multi-use in winter, while dirt trails are ski-only.

Mi. 0.0 Leave the Chester Creek trail at mile 4.6, turning left (north) to cross the bridge over Northern Lights Boulevard. Continue on the pavement.

Mi. 0.3 Turn right at a "T" and pass a low area. Veer right into the woods and cross a wooden bridge.

Mi. 0.7 At another "T" intersection, go right and cross another bridge. (To the left and up a hill just over a tenth of a mile are the chalet and parking lot for the trails

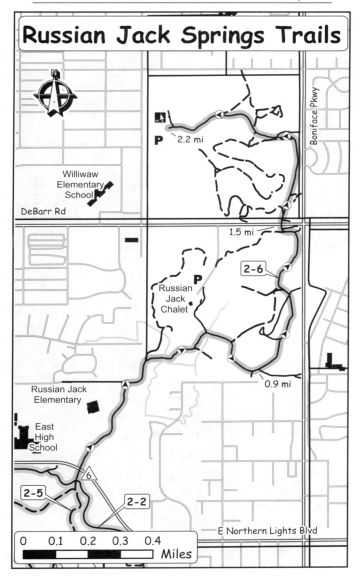

Russian Jack Springs Trails

Boniface Pkwy

2.2 mi

Williwaw
Elementary
School

DeBarr Rd

1.5 mi

2-6

Russian
Jack
Chalet

P

0.9 mi

Russian Jack
Elementary

East
High
School

6

2-5

2-2

E Northern Lights Blvd

| 0 | 0.1 | 0.2 | 0.3 | 0.4 |

Miles

and the golf course, accessed from DeBarr Road.) Follow the paved route. The lights along the trails are for evening skiing.

Mi. 0.9 Continue straight. (To the right you can follow the pavement and ride under Boniface Parkway and on to Nunaka Valley Park.)

Mi. 1.0 At a stop sign turn right and ride on the single-lane park road.

Mi. 1.2 Cross the inbound single-lane road and re-enter the trail at a signpost that points out the "11 Lighted Loop." Continue on this paved route, passing a picnic area to the left. (If you turn left off the trail near the picnic area, you'll find some singletracks and wider trails going into the woods.)

Mi. 1.5 Veer right and ride through a tunnel under DeBarr Road, continuing straight on the pavement up a couple of hills to get a view of the Chugach Mountains to the east, then begin a left-curving descent.

Mi. 1.8 Continue straight and ride past two right turns, both of which lead to an off-leash dog area. (To the right the trail takes you to DeBarr Road. If you then turn left onto the Boniface Parkway street-side path, after one mile you'll intersect the Glenn Highway Trail.)

Mi. 2.2 Arrive at the playing fields. To the left are the softball fields; to the right is a playground, a picnic shelter and tennis courts. (Check out the squirrels at the shelter.) The trail ends at the parking lot, accessed from Pine Street.

Note

You may have noticed a gravel route just after passing under DeBarr Road. During most of the summer, the area is busy with Girl Scout activities. To reduce conflicts while the camp is in use, you should save your dirt-trail riding for the routes south of DeBarr.

There are numerous dirt trails to explore south of DeBarr. Just remember to stay off the golf course and away from boggy areas.

**Getting to the Trailhead:
Russian Jack Chalet Alternative**

To drive to the trailhead from downtown, go east (toward the mountains) on 15th Avenue (the name changes to DeBarr at Lake Otis) from Gambell Street (the Seward Highway). Drive 2.5 miles to Pine Street. Continue straight on DeBarr and turn right before the crest of the hill. Drive past the greenhouse and park near the chalet. The trail entrance is to the left, near the golf course, and in one tenth of a mile joins the route description at mile 0.7. If you're driving from Muldoon Road on the eastern edge of town, go west on DeBarr past Boniface Parkway and turn left at mile 1.8 to reach the parking lot.

Northeast of the Anchorage Bowl

These two routes take riders northeast of the Anchorage Bowl. The first, the Glenn Highway Trail, is a fine commuting route for cyclists riding between Anchorage and Chugiak. The second, a road ride, leaves the Glenn Highway Trail to take riders on a fairly level paved road. It then gives riders a challenging climb on a gravel road. The scenic views and long descent are your rewards.

2-7   Glenn Highway Trail

Difficulty: Easy to moderate, depending on distance. Gravel on steep hills on either side of the Eagle River bridge can be a hazard. Use caution at street crossings.

Surface: Paved.

Winter: Not maintained.

Distance: Up to 37 miles round trip.

The Glenn Highway Trail is one of the first paved trails to clear in the spring, allowing riders to enjoy some early season riding that is off the roadway. It is a good commuting route between the Anchorage Bowl and the communities to the northeast. The only downsides to the route are the noise and fumes from the busy highway. If you like to ride with tunes, this is the place. Just remember to keep to the right of the trail and be alert for other trail users. The route is usually windy in one direction, so pack a jacket.

Many cyclists start this ride near Bartlett High School and the interchange of Muldoon Road and the Glenn Highway. The beginning of the trail is actually farther west at Davis Park in the Mountain View neighborhood. Some amenities of the area include a large playground and picnic area at the Mountain View Lions Community Park, just south of Davis Park. For parents pulling kids in trailers, it's a great place for the little ones to burn off some energy or have a snack before heading home. You can also access the trail from Boniface Parkway by riding through a tunnel.

Good access points along the way include Eagle River Loop Road next to the landfill, downtown Eagle River, and Birchwood Loop Road for those headed toward Anchorage.

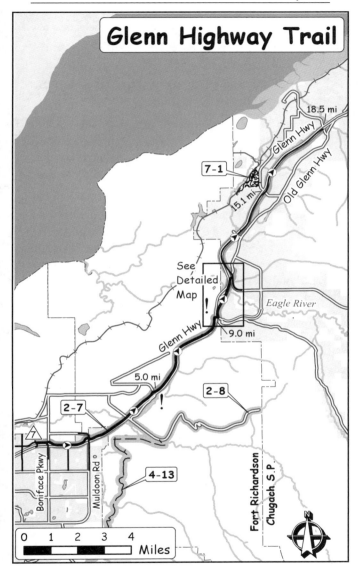

Glenn Highway Trail

Most of the route is straightforward, but there are a few places where you leave the trail and cross roads, so pay close attention to the signs and map.

Mi. 0.0 Ride east from Davis Park, following signs that direct you toward Eagle River.

Mi. 0.3 Pass a tunnel on the right that leads south to Boniface Parkway and continue straight, through a tunnel under Boniface. The trail runs close to the highway, then veers away to make room for the Muldoon Road on-ramp.

Mi. 1.9 Ride into the tunnel under Muldoon. The trail emerges from the tunnel at the 2-mile marker. Veer right. (Left goes to the Alaska Native Heritage Center, Bartlett High School and Elmendorf Air Force Base.) On your right, you'll pass a pullout with a bench. Ride past a tunnel under the highway, which leads to Muldoon Road. Continue straight, following the signs for Eagle River.

Mi. 3.4 Cross Ship Creek on a wooden bridge. Watch for sand and glass on the path. There can be a little ice in early spring.

Mi. 4.5 A large American flag is displayed at the top of a rise.

Mi. 5.0 Pass the 5-mile mark, to arrive at the road that leads to the Fort Richardson main gate. Use caution crossing this road. The continuation of the trail is directly across the road. To the left is the gate; to the right is Arctic Valley Road (Route 2-8).

Mi. 6.4 Pass a bench on the left, then note the Alaska National Guard building farther off the trail.

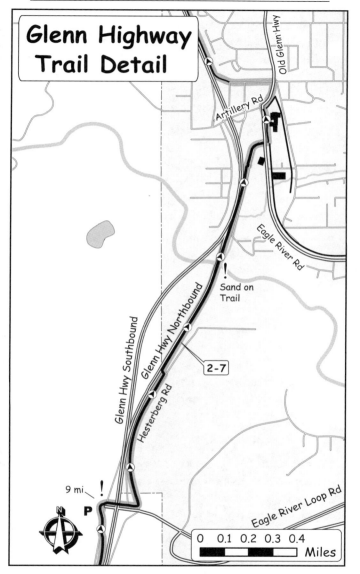

Glenn Highway
Trail Detail

Old Glenn Hwy

Artillery Rd

Eagle River Rd

Sand on
Trail

Glenn Hwy Southbound

Glenn Hwy Northbound

Hesterberg Rd

2-7

9 mi

P

Eagle River Loop Rd

0   0.1 0.2 0.3 0.4
Miles

N

Mi. 8.0   Arrive at a weigh station. This area can be busy with people walking dogs, families with children, and other cyclists. Slow down here and watch for cars entering a gravel parking area. Descend into a quieter area, sheltered by trees. In springtime, this area takes longer to be free from snow and ice. Soon you'll climb and approach a road.

Mi. 9.0   Arrive at Eagle River Loop Road. A small gravel parking area is on the left. Beyond that is the gate to the landfill. Cross the road and follow the trail east, crossing the southbound off-ramp, the Glenn bridge and the northbound on-ramp. On a clear day, you may be able to see Denali and the Talkeetna Mountains to the north.

Mi. 9.2   Turn left onto Hesterberg Road. The trail signs will point left here. Be sure to ride on the right side of the road, with traffic. Signs for a campground and a correctional center also point the way. The road descends toward the trail.

Mi. 9.8   Use caution to cross the road and re-enter the trail to the left. (If you arrive at the correctional center, you went too far.) Descend to a bridge crossing Eagle River. This part of the trail often has sand on it, so use care. The trail then climbs out of the river valley.

Mi. 10.7   The trail follows VFW Road, toward the community of Eagle River.

Mi. 10.9   Cross Eagle River Road, where VFW Road intersects, then turn left onto a street-side trail. A school is on the right. The trail is somewhat rough from tree roots pushing up the pavement.

Mi. 11.0   The trail splits, and you'll go straight, crossing Artillery Road (Old Glenn Highway) at the stoplight. Turn right on the path, following the trail signs. At the next intersection, turn left to ride on Brooks Drive to the next section of the trail. (Continue straight past Brooks to reach the retail district of Eagle River.)

Mi. 11.3 A curve in the road goes left, while the trail goes straight. Use caution here on loose gravel on the edge of the road and the trail. The trail turns sharply to the right, then follows the highway north.

Mi. 12.8 To the right, you'll have a view of Mount Baldy as you approach a motor sports shop.

Mi. 13.0 Turn left to ride through a tunnel. (Going straight will take you into Eagle River.)

Mi. 13.7 Ride past Fire Lake, a float-plane lake surrounded by homes.

Mi. 14.4 Ride past the sign welcoming you to Chugiak, then descend and continue as the trail runs nearer to the off-ramp.

Mi. 15.1 At South Birchwood Loop Road cross the road and continue straight. (Turn left to go to Chugiak High School and ride the ski trails there.) For the next three miles, you'll ride past an area that is more heavily wooded, part of the Elmendorf Moraine, followed by Loretta French Park.

Mi. 18.5 The trail curves away from the highway as you arrive at North Birchwood Loop Road. You can return to Anchorage from here or turn right to arrive at the Old Glenn Highway.

From the intersection of North Birchwood Loop and the Old Glenn, it's about 5.1 miles to Thunderbird Falls and 5.4 miles to the beginning of Eklutna Lake Road. Another 10 miles will take you to the lake. (See Route 7-3 for more information.) The roads are narrow and the route does require some highway riding. The strong-legged can also climb to the Peters Creek Trail from here.

2-8 Arctic Valley Road Hill Climb

Difficulty: Moderate to difficult with a sustained climb and descent on a mountain road.

Surface: Paved and gravel, often washboard surface.

Winter: Not recommended.

Distance: 17.6 miles round trip.

Arctic Valley Road offers riders some early season dirt hill climbing with the benefit of some beautiful viewpoints overlooking Anchorage and the Ship Creek Valley. For riders compelled to hike or who enjoy fall berry picking after riding up the road, Arctic Valley offers a short steep hike to a ridge line and a season's worth of berry picking.

The road takes you from the Glenn Highway, through part of Fort Richardson Military Reservation, and up a steep mountain road, ending at a downhill ski area. The last five-plus miles are gravel, so you'll want your mountain bike for this one. The road can be very dusty and has several areas with a washboard surface.

For a good warmup before the climb, begin at Bartlett High School, just northwest of where Muldoon Road meets the Glenn Highway. Take the bike path toward the Glenn, then keep left to ride the Glenn Highway Trail out of Anchorage. Just past the 5-mile marker, where the trail intersects the main road out of Fort Richardson, turn right onto the road.

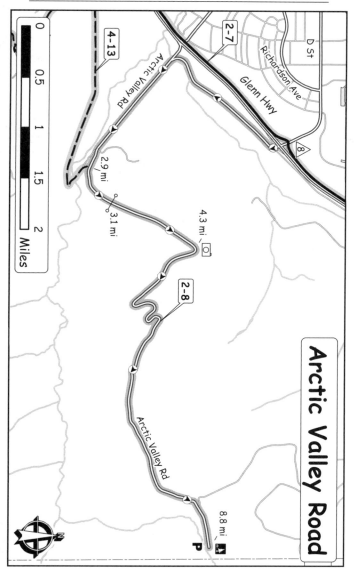

Arctic Valley Road

Mi. 0.0 From the road, ride east, past the off-ramp from the highway. The route curves right and roughly parallels the highway. Be aware that traffic leaving the highway does not stop.

Mi. 1.5 Arrive at a stop sign and turn left. (Traffic coming from the right is exiting the Glenn Highway at the first exit for Arctic Valley Road. Because the Glenn is closed to bikes, you shouldn't ride it to get here.) Ride past a driving range for the Moose Run Country Club.

Mi. 2.3 Pass the golf course parking lot. The road will begin to climb.

Mi. 2.9 Continue on the road as you pass the parking area for the Snowhawk Cabin on the right. (Turn right here to take the Bulldog (Tank) Trail to Far North Bicentennial Park, Route 4-12.) Pass another parking area and a building on the left.

Mi. 3.1 The pavement ends and the climbing becomes more challenging on the washboard surface. You'll pass a gate with a sign noting the gate closes at 10:00 p.m. The military police lock the gate each evening.

Mi. 3.9 Pass a pullout on the right, which is the end of a double-track trail that descends the mountain. (You must check in with the RAP system before riding off the road. See Resources for more information.)

Mi. 4.3 A wide area in the road allows you to pull over to the left side and look out over the city. Another overlook is just up the road, on the right.

Mi. 5.0 A pullout on the right offers an entrance to the double track listed earlier.

Mi. 5.3   An emergency telephone is on the left side of the road, where a power line crosses over the roadway. Ride up a left-turning switchback to an overlook on the left side of the road. The road then curves right.

Mi. 6.8   Another pullout is on the right.

Mi. 7.3   From this point, you'll get your first view of the ski area.

Mi. 7.9   An emergency phone is on the right. Arrive at a parking area on the right that is also a hiking trailhead. Note the view of Ship Creek Valley from here.

Mi. 8.5   As the road splits, stay to the left and make the final push to the trailhead fee station at the end of the road.

Mi. 8.8   A parking lot is on the left. If you still have energy in your legs, you can hike from here up Rendezvous Peak. The hiking trails are off-limits to bikes, so you'll need to lock and stash it before making the trek. The parking area and other facilities are maintained by the nonprofit Anchorage Ski Club. If you drive to the trailhead, deposit your fee here. Annual parking permits are also available through the club. See Resources for more information.

The Cold War–era Nike missile site north of the parking area is on military land and is presently off-limits. A firing range is nearby and bullets can ricochet toward it. Posted signs and fencing are frequently vandalized so be aware that you should still keep out. The site is listed on the National Register of Historic Places but has deteriorated over the years. The Army is trying to determine whether to raze the site or renovate it because of its historical status.

Option

To get to Arctic Valley Road by way of the Bulldog (Tank) Trail, see Route 4-13. Just after mile 8.6 of that route, you'll arrive at mile 2.9 of Arctic Valley Road. Turn right to climb.

If you plan to leave the road to ride any side trails or the Bulldog Trail or to hike on Army land, you must check in using the RAP system. See Resources for more information.

Chapter 3

Kincaid Park

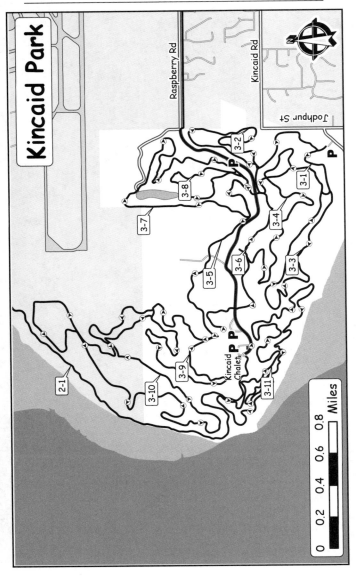

Kincaid Park has a network of more than 30 miles of dirt trails for summer riding. This park of nearly 1,500 acres was developed as a cross-country ski area, so most trails are rather wide and very hilly. This makes the climbs more challenging than trails that are designed along contours. Many routes have a single heavily used dirt path running down the center or on either side of the trails. This is the popular line most mountain bikers use.

Kincaid has a few singletrack trails, some of which are used almost exclusively by mountain bikers looking for more challenging trails, for variety or for shortcuts. It also has trails that fall between these widths. This variety makes Kincaid Park a good place for riders of all skill levels.

Trail conditions vary throughout the riding season, which officially begins on June 1. With a few exceptions, the trails dry out early and the soils drain well after a rain. Later in the summer, in the days after a rain, be aware that the hard-packed dirt line of the trail can be slick due to moss growing on the surface. The moss is difficult to see, but it is very common on the Mize Loop. During dry years, some trails have sand-filled ruts. Loss of traction makes these trails more difficult to ride.

Trails are maintained primarily by the Nordic Skiing Association of Anchorage. The NSAA keeps the trails groomed for skiing and makes improvements, including the addition of lighting. All of Kincaid Park, with the exception of the Tony Knowles Coastal Trail and the park road, is off-limits to winter cycling once the ski trail grooming begins. In the autumn, before the snow falls, the lit trails offer some fun evening rides, and the birch trees in the park make autumn riding on crisp sunny days even more spectacular.

Kincaid has a large moose population, and bears are sometimes seen in the park during the summer. Lynx, porcupine, hares, owls and bald eagles are just some of the other animals you may encounter when riding. Take time to learn about bear and moose behavior before venturing onto the trails.

Trailheads

Kincaid has five designated trailheads, accessible by car or bicycle. You can also bike to the park on the Coastal Trail.

Getting Here by Car

There are five main parking lots. Park hours are from 8 a.m. to 11 p.m., but the gates are open only from 10 a.m. to 10 p.m.

Raspberry Road: From southbound Minnesota Drive, take the Raspberry Road exit and go right, heading west. Drive 3.5 miles on Raspberry and enter the park. The Raspberry parking lot is on the right at mile 3.9. This is the only parking area outside the park gates.

Little Campbell Lake: Upon entering the park at mile 3.5 of Raspberry Road, turn right onto a gravel road. The parking lot is at mile 4.1.

Stadium: Continue past the Raspberry parking lot, where you'll pass a gate (note what time the gate is locked nightly). After a second gate, the Stadium parking lot is on the right at mile 5.1.

Chalet: To park at the Kincaid Chalet, continue to the end of Raspberry Road and turn right into the parking area. The chalet has the only public restrooms in the park.

Jodhpur: From South Anchorage, take Dimond Boulevard west. Just one mile past the intersection of Jewel Lake Road and Dimond Boulevard, you'll arrive at Sand Lake Road. After Sand Lake, the road curves right and becomes Jodhpur Street. At 2.2 miles, turn left into the park entrance. The parking lot to the right is the trailhead for biking, hiking and skiing. If you continue straight on the park road, you'll arrive at the parking lot for the motocross area. Note the gate closing time before you begin riding.

Note

Had you continued another 0.4 mile north on Jodhpur Street, you would have arrived at a small parking area on the left, where the Tree Tunnel enters the park.

Getting Here by Bicycle

Ride the Tony Knowles Coastal Trail (Route 2-1) to the park and enter the dirt trails on the Sisson Loop (Route 3-10) or after reaching the chalet. The Coastal Trail begins downtown, just north of Elderberry Park on 2nd Avenue.

To enter the park from the east, ride the bike path along the south side of Raspberry Road. It is legal for you to ride on Raspberry Road if you follow the same rules as a motorized vehicle. If you're coming from South Anchorage, take Dimond Boulevard and stay on the bike path until you reach Sand Lake Road, where you can ride on the road to Jodhpur Street to get to the Jodhpur trailhead.

Using the Trail Descriptions

Trail markings throughout Kincaid Park refer to the direction of travel for skiing the routes. This guide mostly follows the posted directions, but occasionally it will travel in the opposite direction. Use caution whenever biking against the flow of traffic and avoid doing so on trails with blind corners, such as Roller Coaster.

Using This Guide at Kincaid

Because Kincaid trails were designed for skiing, they have lots of steep ups and downs. Many intersections are at the bottoms of hills, so it's easy for a fast mountain biker to miss them. If you stop to check your map, you may have to start your next climb with no momentum. When using this guide, read the descriptions, check the map and make a mental note of the route before you start. Save the map-checking for the top of the next hill.

Because Kincaid Park's trails are composed of loops, you can link together several of the routes presented here to make a grand tour of the park. See how many miles you can cover without repeating any trails and you'll gain an appreciation for why the park is so popular.

Remember that Kincaid is open for biking in the summer months only, normally by June 1. Once the trails are being groomed for skiing, they are off-limits. The Coastal Trail, however, is a multi-use route in winter. You can expect the trails to have snow by mid- to late October, but this varies from one year to the next.

Jodhpur and Horseshoe Loops

3-1   Jodhpur Loop

Difficulty: Easy.

Surface: Wide and grassy.

Distance: 2.2-mile loop.

This easy loop includes some shortcuts and alternative trails for exploring in the southeast section of the park. Begin at the north corner of the Jodhpur parking lot, near a kiosk opposite the lot entrance. Enter the trails at the wooden trailhead bollards.

Mi. 0.0   At the bollards ride straight and enter the woods.

Mi. 0.1   Stay left for the longest route. (Going straight and down a hill will lop off a major loop, but it offers a shortcut if you want to quickly reach Raspberry Road.)

Mi. 0.4   Keep right to stay on the main trail. (Left goes to steeper trails, such as Ice Box.)

Mi. 0.5   Stay right. (The Wall enters from the left.)

Mi. 0.8   Go straight to take the longest route, up Moose Hill, which ends with a fast descent. (Many riders go left at the 0.8 mile point, cutting off a good part of the loop.) Go past the first right you encounter at mile 1.2 and descend to another intersection.

Mi. 1.2   Go right to keep moving forward on the loop. (Straight will take you to Four Corners and Big Dipper, Route 3-4; left will return you to the parking lot.)

Mi. 1.3   Go left and climb, then turn right. Ride toward the bridge over Raspberry Road, but turn right instead of going over the bridge.

Mi. 1.4 Go over a slight rise, then ride a fast descent. At the bottom of the hill you have several options: continue on Jodhpur, ride Horseshoe (Route 3-2), or take a shortcut out of the park.

Mi. 1.5 Go right to continue on the loop. (If you want to add Horseshoe Loop to the ride, keep straight.) Climb a gradual hill and follow the route to Burky's Bend.

Mi. 2.0 Stay on the main route at Burky's. (A cutoff to the right leads onto a narrower route and some short singletrack connectors to Moose Hill.) Make a final descent.

Mi. 2.1 Go right as you enter an open area and approach an information sign. Turn left at the sign to return to the parking lot.

Mi. 2.2 Arrive at the parking lot.

Option

To ride the Jodhpur Loop without Moose Hill, at 0.8 mile stay on the most heavily used route as it curves left. At just over 0.1 mile down the trail, Moose Hill rejoins from the right. Stay straight to continue the ride.

3-2 Horseshoe Loop

Difficulty: Moderate with steep climbs and narrower trail.

Surface: Mostly grass with some roots and dirt.

Distance: 1.6-mile loop.

Prepare for some steep climbs and fast descents on the Horseshoe Loop. This trail is narrower than many in the park, but not as narrow as singletrack. During the middle of summer some sections get overgrown with cow parsnip

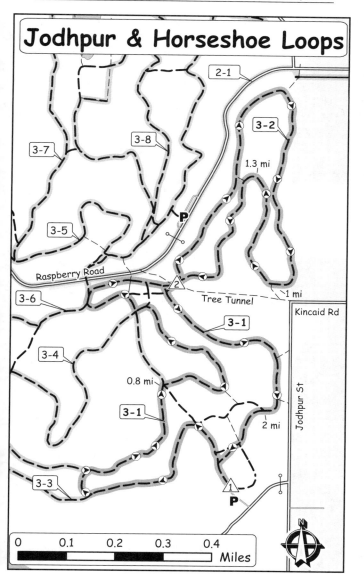

Jodhpur & Horseshoe Loops

or other foliage.

A few singletrack trails branch off the Horseshoe Loop. Some have been adopted by more adventurous mountain bikers, but because they cross onto land that is outside the park boundary, they haven't been included in this guide. The only major intersections involve a shortcut, so the route is easy to follow.

The intersection of Jodhpur and Horseshoe is marked with a sign directing you to the right for Jodhpur and left for Horseshoe. But it's an easy place to take a wrong turn because another trail, which is not on information signs, meets here as well. The route is known as the Tree Tunnel and takes you out of the park to the intersection of Jodhpur Street and Kincaid Road.

Ride left of the sign toward Horseshoe Loop. You'll see three trail choices. Take the leftmost option. (To the right is the end of the trail; farther right is Tree Tunnel.)

Mi. 0.0 Enter the trail just after mile 1.5 of the Jodhpur Loop ride.

Mi. 0.2 Keep straight. (To the right is a shortcut to mile 1.3.)

Mi. 0.5 Stay straight, on the main route. (A singletrack drops to the left into the woods.) After a few more challenging climbs, you may glimpse a white water tank in the trees to the left as you approach the 1.0-mile mark. Climb a short hill and descend.

Mi. 1.0 Stay straight. (A singletrack to the left at the bottom of the short descent connects to Tree Tunnel. By mid-July this connector route is often overgrown with devil's club and cow parsnip.)

Mi. 1.3 Keep riding straight. (The mile 0.2 shortcut rejoins the main trail from the right.)

Mi. 1.6 Horseshoe Loop ends. To your immediate right is where you began; to your left is Tree Tunnel. Go straight, passing Tree Tunnel, then turn left to reconnect with Jodhpur.

Jodhpur and Horseshoe via Rasberry Trailhead

You can easily access the Jodhpur and Horseshoe loops from the Raspberry trailhead.

Mi. 0.0 Starting at the Raspberry trailhead map and information sign, go left and descend. Go straight, staying roughly parallel to the road. As you begin a steep climb, stay right and arrive at an intersection at the top of the hill. A sign points left toward the Jodhpur trailhead.

Mi. 0.2 Turn left and cross the bridge over Raspberry Road.

Mi. 0.3 Turn left at the sign for the Jodhpur Loop (mile 1.4 of the route) and descend to the intersection of several trails. Here you'll see a map to help you find the routes for Jodhpur and Horseshoe loops.

Tree Tunnel Option

The Tree Tunnel is just over a quarter-mile long. The singletrack connector to Horseshoe Loop is just past mile 0.2 when riding out of the park, making this a convenient shortcut to the road.

Kincaid Hills

South of Raspberry Road, in the center of Kincaid Park, is a set of trails you can access only from other routes. The trails don't have names, but points along the trails are named for the unique features of each particular spot. The routes are known for the long steep hills and slightly narrower riding surface, relative to other Kincaid trails.

3-3 Ice Box, Hair Pin, Mize's Folly, The Wall

Difficulty: Moderate to difficult, with steep hills and some loose sand.

Surface: Midwidth trail, mostly grassy with a dirt line.

Distance: 2.5 miles one way.

The center of the park, on the south side of Raspberry Road, features a collection of challenging climbs and some longer descents. The ride descriptions begin on the Jodhpur Loop, but you can easily access them from other trails.

The ride to Ice Box and Hair Pin begins at mile 0.4 of Jodhpur Loop (Route 3-1).

Mi. 0.0 Turn left at the Intersection of Jodhpur and Ice Box and begin a gentle climb through stands of mature cottonwood and devil's club. (You may hear dirt bikes using the motocross area not far from this trail.)

Mi. 0.1 A sign warns of a steep descent.

Mi. 0.2 Stay straight as you ride past the intersection that goes to the right and leads to Four Corners and the bridge. A sign reading "Ice Box" marks the bottom of the hill.

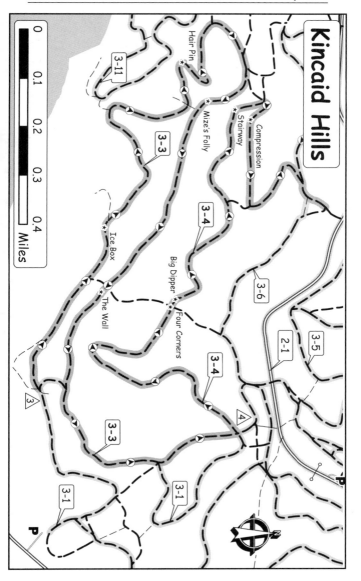

Kincaid Hills

Mi. 0.4 A steep singletrack on the slope to the left joins the trail. Be aware of riders coming down this hill who may not be prepared to stop. From Ice Box, the main trail climbs, arriving at a meadow.

Mi. 0.6 Another warning sign announces a steep descent. After the descent, you'll climb.

Mi. 0.8 The trail will level out for a moment and you'll see the next climb, Hair Pin.

Mi. 1.1 Go right toward Mize's Folly and Compression. (Turning left connects you with the Lekisch Trail System, Route 3-11, and is the shortest route to the Stadium.)

Mi. 1.2 Stay right at the next two intersections.

Mi. 1.3 Go right for Mize's Folly. (Left goes to the end of Stairway and to Compression.)

Mize's Folly begins with an immediate steep descent. Watch for loose sand in some places, especially on a left curve. After the curve, you can build up speed to climb a short hill.

Mi. 1.5 The terrain evens out to a moderate, rolling descent before dropping more steeply.

Mi. 1.8 Continue straight where the trail splits. (Left would take you on a shortcut to Four Corners and on to the bridge.) Stay straight again as the shortcut crosses the trail, then begin a steep climb known as The Wall. The terrain will level then gradually descend to rejoin Jodhpur.

Mi. 2.0 Turn left to take Jodhpur to Big Dipper and Stairway to Heaven.

Mi. 2.3 Stay left on Jodhpur. (If you go straight you'll ride the Moose Hill portion of Jodhpur Loop, adding a little more distance to the ride.)

Mi. 2.5 As you're descending, notice a footpath into the woods on the left. You may be able to see a rusted car that was abandoned years ago. Turn left at a four-way intersection to begin Big Dipper and Stairway. (Right is the exit of Moose Hill; straight goes to the bridge.)

3-4 Big Dipper, Stairway to Heaven, Compression

Difficulty: Moderate to difficult with steep climbs and descents.

Surface: Grass surface with a single dirt line.

Distance: 1.6 miles one way.

The Big Dipper and Stairway to Heaven segments of trail offer riding terrain similar to the Ice Box area. The mileage presented here is independent of the previous ride, but linked together with the Jodhpur Loop these routes make for a fun, challenging outing.

Mi. 0.0 Start at mile 1.2 of the Jodhpur Loop and ride straight (when leaving the Moose Hill portion of that trail), following the sign for Big Dipper. The route climbs immediately and offers a couple of ups and downs. Stay on the main route.

Mi. 0.4 The trail descends then levels off.

Mi. 0.6 Arrive at Four Corners and continue straight. (Left goes toward The Wall and Ice Box; right goes to the bridge over Raspberry Road.)

Mi. 0.9 Continue straight for Stairway. (Turning right takes you to the end of Compression and on to Margaux's

Loop, Route 3-6.) A final climb up the steepest part of Stairway goes through a patch of cow parsnip. Steer away from the plant as much as possible when it's in full flower to avoid a reaction that can cause blisters.

Mi. 1.2 Turn right at the top of the climb to reach Compression. (Left goes to Mize's Folly; straight, then right goes to Lower Tunnel and Dark Alley.) Looking east, from the top of Compression, you'll see the distinct jagged triangle shaped summit of O'Malley Peak. Be aware that the dirt line can get rutted on this fast downhill. Riding on the grass is slower, but it can also be rutty. Use caution and know your limits. After the descent, you'll have two small climbs.

Mi. 1.4 Turn left. (Right connects back to the top of Big Dipper.)

Mi. 1.6 After a short descent, merge onto Margaux's Loop. Use caution entering this trail. As you approach the next intersection, you can choose where you want to go next. Use routes 3-6 and 3-1 to return to the Jodhpur parking lot, or use this description to reach the stadium via Roller Coaster, where you can ride other loops:

Go straight. (Right takes you on a shortcut to stay on Margaux's and ride to the bridge.)

Mi. 1.7 Ride through the Upper Tunnel, under Raspberry Road, and take the first left to reach Roller Coaster.

Mi. 1.9 Turn left and cross a gravel road, then follow the Roller Coaster back to the Stadium (see Route 3-5 for complete description).

Margaux's Loop

Margaux's Loop connects the Raspberry trailhead to the Stadium. The route on the north side of Raspberry Road is the westbound half of the loop. South of the road is the eastbound half. When combined, they make up one of the most popular loops in the park, leading to several other trails. Use Margaux's to access your favorite routes and the chalet.

3-5   Rasberry Parking Lot to Stadium via Margaux's Loop

Difficulty: Easy to moderate with hills and blind corners.

Surface: Wide, grassy tread.

Distance: 1.6 miles one way.

Margaux's Loop is one of the most popular routes in the park, mostly because of a stretch called Roller Coaster. This gravity-fueled trail gives riders a rolling, twisting descent reminiscent of an amusement park ride, often complete with the whoops and screams. Margaux's is also popular because it begins at the only trailhead that is outside of the park gates and leads to so many other trails.

Begin at the Raspberry parking lot.

Mi. 0.0   Start at the trailhead map and information sign, go left and descend. Go straight, staying roughly parallel to the road. As you begin a steep climb, stay right until you reach an intersection at the top of the hill.

Mi. 0.2   Go right to ride Margaux's Loop. (Straight is a singletrack that lops off a portion of Margaux's Loop. Left takes you south of Raspberry Road.)

Mi. 0.4 Stay straight, riding past the singletrack as it rejoins Margaux's from the left.

Mi. 0.6 Continue straight. You may notice the road to the left as you pedal up Burky's Climb.

Mi. 0.9 Veer left at a meadow and go straight.

Mi. 1.0 Cross a park road (a gate is on the left) and ride Roller Coaster. After the trail levels, continue straight, past Dark Alley.

Mi. 1.5 Go straight. (A right onto Tasha's Turn leads to Mize Loop and Elliott's Climb.)

Mi. 1.6 Arrive at the north end of the Stadium.

3-5 Stadium to Raspberry Parking Lot via Margaux's Loop

Difficulty: Easy to moderate with some steep hills.

Surface: Wide, grassy tread.

Distance: 1.6 miles one way.

The Stadium is the staging area for bike, running and ski races, and several trails converge here. The Kincaid Chalet, with restrooms and information, is on the other side of the Stadium, just up the hill. This ride begins at the Stadium parking lot.

Mi. 0.0 Begin at the information sign and map at the north end of the Stadium parking lot and ride down a gentle slope toward the tile and cement benches and table of Margaux's memorial. Veer right as you approach the memorial and make a short climb before taking the steep, sometimes rutted, descent. The trail veers right and climbs again.

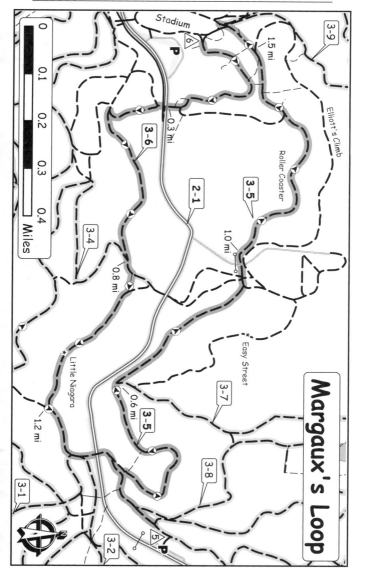

Margaux's Loop

Stadium

P

3-9

1.5 mi

Elliott's Climb

0.3 mi

3-6

Roller Coaster

2-1

3-5

1.0 mi

3-4

0.8 mi

Little Niagara

1.2 mi

Easy Street

0.6 mi

3-7

3-5

3-1

3-8

3-2

5

P

0 0.1 0.2 0.3 0.4 Miles

81

Mi. 0.3 Stay straight. (Left goes to Dark Alley and the end of Roller Coaster.) Ride through the Lower Tunnel.

Mi. 0.4 After the tunnel, go straight. (The skiing direction would take you to the right, but most cyclists go straight.)

Mi. 0.5 Make a sharp left turn to stay on Margaux's, then arrive at Mountain View.

Mi. 0.7 Just after the sign reading "Mt View Top of the Form," you'll descend.

Mi. 0.8 Be alert to riders merging onto the trail from the right, then take the next right, a steep shortcut on a well-worn route. (Straight will take you to the Upper Tunnel or to the main route of Margaux's Loop, where you would turn right.)

Mi. 0.9 Go right to rejoin the main trail on the descent. Be aware that riders on the main route are also descending and may not see you!

Mi. 1.0 Approach the steep descent known as Little Niagara. The trail surface can be sandy and loose, especially in dry years, so you may want to approach on the outside to get more control. Depending on your skill and the trail conditions, you may get enough speed on this descent to coast up the next hill.

Mi. 1.2 Stay left to continue on Margaux's and reach the bridge. (Right goes to Four Corners.)

Mi. 1.3 Keep left and cross the bridge. (Right goes to Jodhpur and Horseshoe loops.) After the bridge, go right to ride to the Raspberry parking lot. (Stay straight to return to the Stadium.)

Mi. 1.4 Go right and descend toward Raspberry. At the bottom of the hill, keep to the right and climb.

Mi. 1.6 At the top of the hill, turn right to enter the parking lot.

Lake Loops

Lake Loop and Inner Lake Loop are located in the northeastern section of the park and take riders to Little Campbell Lake. Both loops feature challenging climbs and descents as they twist through the area.

3-7 Lake Loop from Margaux's Loop

Difficulty: Moderate with steep climbs and descents.

Surface: Somewhat narrow, mostly grassy tread.

Distance: 2.9-mile loop.

The Lake Loop features some steeper climbs and descents than some other park trails. A visit to Little Campbell Lake can be one of the highlights of this ride before you return to the trailhead. This route gives you the option to take a longer ride by warming up with some trails that are a little more moderate. The mileage used here is for the Lake Loop on its own, starting at the Raspberry parking lot. (You can also start the ride at the Little Campbell Lake trailhead.)

Mi. 0.0 Starting at the Raspberry trailhead map and information sign, go left and descend. Go straight, staying roughly parallel to the road. As you begin a steep climb, stay right until you reach an intersection at the top of the hill.

Mi. 0.2 Go right to ride Margaux's Loop. (Straight is

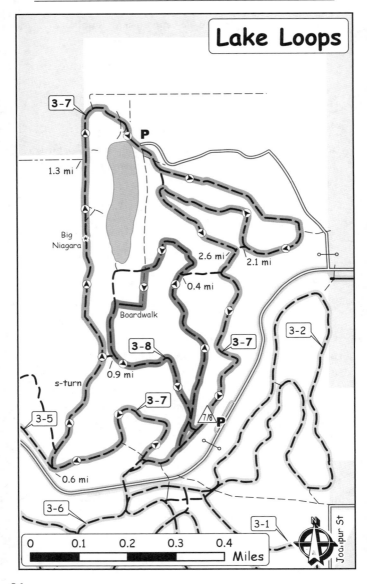

Lake Loops

1.3 mi

Big Niagara

2.6 mi

2.1 mi

0.4 mi

Boardwalk

3-8

3-7

3-2

0.9 mi

s-turn

3-5

3-7

7/8 P

0.6 mi

3-6

3-1

Jodhpur St

N

| 0 | 0.1 | 0.2 | 0.3 | 0.4 |
Miles

a singletrack that lops off a portion of Margaux's Loop. Left takes you south of Raspberry Road.)

Mi. 0.4 Stay straight, riding past the singletrack that rejoins Margaux's from the left.

Mi. 0.6 Make a 90-degree right turn onto S-Turn. (If you miss the turn, you'll begin a gradual climb.) After taking the right, you'll start descending.

Option

To make this ride longer, at the 0.6-mile point, continue straight up Burky's Climb.

Mi. 0.9 Veer right as you enter a meadow. Keep right to ride Easy Street. Easy Street ends when it meets S-Turn. Go left here to continue toward Lake Loop.

To make the ride longer still, after Burky's continue on to Roller Coaster as follows:

Mi. 0.9 Veer left at the meadow.

Mi. 1.0 Cross a park road (gate is on the left) and ride Roller Coaster.

Mi. 1.5 Go right on Tasha's Turn. Follow the route as it curves to the right.

Mi. 1.8 Veer right onto Elliott's Climb.

Mi. 2.3 Cross the park road again, returning to the meadow where the trail curves left.

Mi. 2.5 Go right onto Easy Street.

Go left onto S-Turn to rejoin the main route.

Mi. 0.6 Keep riding straight as you pass the intersection with Easy Street (see option box).

Mi. 0.8 At the bottom of the hill continue straight to ride the Lake Loop. (A right turn would take you to the Inner Lake Loop.) After the intersection the trail immediately climbs, gives a short reprieve, then climbs again. The next descent is known as Big Niagara. Caution: Watch for erosion before you start down Big Niagara so you can pick the best line. You'll climb and get another descent, before following a fence line.

Option

Mi. 1.3 A trail connecting to Arlene's Way, off the Mize Loop, is on the left. You'll see it as you approach a fence line. The route follows a fence and takes you up a couple of steep climbs and descents before meeting Arlene's. Turn left to reach the Mize Loop. While popular for racers, the fence line route isn't heavily used and can get overgrown in late summer, covering obstacles and ruts. Use caution on this trail.

Mi. 1.5 Arrive at the parking lot for Little Campbell Lake. Ride across the lot and cross a paved path that leads to the dock. Go to the left into the woods and up the hill.

Mi. 1.6 Stay left as the trail splits.

Mi. 2.1 Stay right at the intersection. (Left is a short-cut.)

Mi. 2.4 Stay left and note that you are again above the lake.

Mi. 2.6 Go right, then left to return to the Raspberry parking lot.

Mi. 2.9 Turn left into the parking lot.

3-8   Inner Lake Loop

Difficulty: Moderate, with hills.

Surface: Narrower with a grassy tread.

Distance: 1.3-mile loop.

The Inner Lake Loop has sections that are a little narrower than the Lake Loop, yet not as narrow as singletrack. It sees less use and is quieter than some more popular routes. You can access it from the Lake Loop, but this description gives the mileage independent of other rides.

Mi. 0.0   Start at the Raspberry trailhead map and information sign. Turn left to descend just a short distance. Before reaching the bottom of the hill, turn right, descending farther into an often grassy part of the trail. To your right, the trail forks. Take the right option for the beginning of the trail. (The left option is where the loop ends.)

Mi. 0.4   Turn left. (If you go straight, you'll connect with Lake Loop just after the 2.6 mile point.) A sweeping curve descends and emerges from the woods at the south shore of Little Campbell Lake.

Mi. 0.7   Go left. (The winter ski trail goes straight, but the area is marshy in summer.) Turn right onto a boardwalk to cross the wet area.

Mi. 0.8   Take a left when you meet the main trail.

Mi. 0.9   Stay left and climb. (To the right is where S-Turn and Lake Loop meet.) A descent just after a sharp right gives you momentum for a climb back to the start of the loop.

Mi. 1.2   Go right, then left to climb back to the main

trail. Take a sharp left to return to the trailhead at the top of the hill.

Mi. 1.3 Turn right into the parking lot to complete the ride.

Mize and Sisson Loops

This pair of trails in the northwestern section of the park offer more moderate terrain and a number of scenic views of Cook Inlet. Sisson Loop is directly beneath a flight path for Ted Stevens Anchorage International Airport, so don't be alarmed by the jets taking off and landing.

3-9   Mize Loop

Difficulty: Easy to moderate with some hills.

Surface: Wide, grassy surface. Dirt line can be slick in late summer.

Distance: 2.8-mile loop.

Mize Loop is a good choice for newer riders or for those wanting to bike a more mellow trail. A few climbs may be challenging for novices and children, but the descents make the route feel shorter than it is. It also has a shortcut where riders can avoid the longest hills. Mize Loop also leads to Sisson Loop, the easiest trail Kincaid Park offers.

This ride begins at the Stadium parking lot.

Mi. 0.0 Begin at the information sign and map at the north end of the parking lot and ride toward the northeast corner of the Stadium, past the start of Margaux's Loop and down a wide gravel and grass route.

Mi. 0.1 Veer right at a split in the trail. (Straight is the end of the loop.)

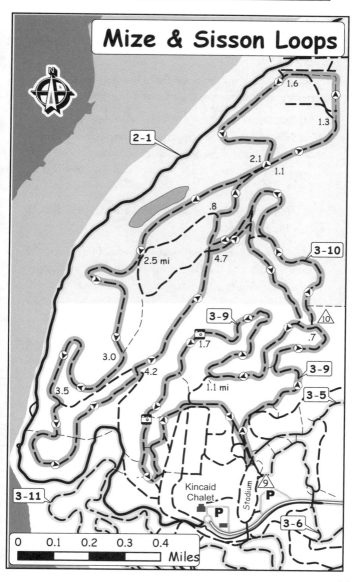

Mi. 0.2   Stay left as Tasha's Turn enters from the right, then veer left down the hill. (To the right is the beginning of Elliott's Climb.)

Mi. 0.3   Stay on the main trail (You may notice a singletrack entering from the right, next to a light pole.)

Mi. 0.7   After passing signs for Sherwood Forest and the archery range, arrive at an intersection, where you continue straight to stay on Mize. (Right are the Sisson Trail, Arlene's Way and the Ski for Women Cutoff, described in Route 3-10.)

Mi. 0.8   Continue straight. (Ski for Women Cutoff rejoins Mize here.)

Mi. 1.1   The main trail curves right. (To the left a shortcut returns to the Stadium.) For the next half mile, the trail rolls though a stand of mature cottonwoods. Cook Inlet comes into view as you approach Pia-Margrethe's Overlook.

Mi. 1.7   A stop at the wooden bench at Pia's offers a view over the park toward the water and the gravel trails and ponds below. Just past the ponds, you may see cyclists riding the Tony Knowles Coastal Trail. From here, Mize Loop continues descending.

Mi. 1.8   Continue straight and pass a shortcut to the left.

Mi. 2.0   At the top of the climb, arrive at grassy Arlene's Overlook. This memorial includes two metal benches that invite you to take time to enjoy the views. The bench to the right looks beyond the trees across the water to Mount Susitna, also known as Sleeping Lady. To the left, tucked off the trail in the trees, the second bench faces Fire Island. Continue on a fast descent, a short climb, and a curve to the left.

Mi. 2.1   Stay left when two options branch off to the right. Enjoy the twisting turns of the route.

Mi. 2.3   Go left as the trail straightens. You may notice the yellow and silver disc golf basket off the trail to the right as you continue.

Mi. 2.4   Stay left, then continue straight as you ride past the end of the mile 1.1 shortcut.

Mi. 2.5   Continue straight on the main trail then climb.

Mi. 2.7   Arrive at the Stadium and veer left to return to the information sign.

Mi. 2.8   End at the information sign.

Option

Add a small slice of singletrack to the beginning of this ride by going right onto Elliott's Climb at mile 0.2. Just before mile 0.3 take a left, descending onto a singletrack. Rejoin Mize by turning right.

3-10   Sisson Loop

Difficulty: Easy to moderate, with a somewhat steep descent and climb to link the route with Mize.

Surface: Surface varies in width and character. Includes singletrack through tall grass, wide gravel sections and dirt.

Distance: 5.2-mile loop, plus Mize Loop or Coastal Trail for access.

Sisson Loop has the easiest terrain in the park, with only a few minor hills. The trail varies from grassy singletrack sections to areas where a road-width gravel trail turns to pavement. It has several access points for riders on the Tony Knowles Coastal Trail, many of which are noted in this description. The numerous cutoffs and access routes can make this trail confusing to ride, but new signs installed in 2004 are helpful. This route begins just after mile 0.7 of the Mize Loop ride.

Mi. 0.0 Turn right at a sign for the Sisson Trail to leave the Mize Loop (Route 3-9). This connector route is known as Arlene's Way. Stay on the main route. (A fence line route enters from the right.)

Mi. 0.4 Veer right. (If you go left here and at the next intersection, you'll return to the Mize Loop. This route is known as the Ski for Women Cutoff, named for the ski race fund-raiser held every year on Super Bowl Sunday.)

Mi. 0.6 Stay right to continue descending and enter an open area.

Mi. 0.8 Stay right of a directional sign, then turn right onto a gravel road–like trail.

Mi. 0.9 Go right at a "T," onto a similar gravel trail.

Mi. 1.0 Continue straight as another trail merges from the left.

Mi. 1.1 Stay on the gravel route. (A grass-surfaced trail enters from the left. This will be part of the return loop.) The surface will turn to pavement as you near an airport fence. The gate is numbered "W5."

Mi. 1.3 Turn left onto a singletrack and ride along the

fence. Ride past gate W4. (Left is a shortcut that takes you away from the fence line.)

Mi. 1.5 The singletrack ends at a gravel trail. Turn left and continue straight as you pass the end of the shortcut.

Mi. 1.6 Veer left to continue on the Sisson Loop. (A right turn leads to mile 8.4 of the Coastal Trail, Route 2-1. This is a good place to hit the dirt when accessing Kincaid via the Coastal Trail.)

Mi. 1.8 Veer left at a split in the trail. (Straight follows a utility corridor that services a water line. It eventually crosses the Coastal Trail.) Stay on the main route as the singletrack takes you through a stand of alders.

Mi. 2.1 Arrive at a gravel trail and turn right. (This is mile 1.1 of the outbound route.) Stay right again as you pass the outbound route on the left.

Mi. 2.2 Continue straight. (A trail climbs to the right.) A small pond ahead is a good spot to see birds and watch moose browsing in the water. Across the pond and uphill, you may notice riders on the Coastal Trail.

Mi. 2.5 After the pond, veer left and climb gradually. Veer right at the split in the trail and descend, then climb.

Mi. 2.7 At the top of the climb, go left at the "T."

Mi. 3.0 Begin a short, somewhat steep descent and keep straight as you pass an incoming trail on the right. Veer right at the next intersection. (Left takes you back to the pond.)

Mi. 3.3 Go left to ride a switchback. (Right is a connector to the previous stretch of trail.)

Mi. 3.5 Go left. (Right goes to the Coastal Trail.)

Turn right at the next two junctions.

Mi. 3.7 Veer left. (Right goes to Coastal Trail.)

Mi. 3.9 Continue straight at a four-way intersection.

Mi. 4.2 Veer left. (Straight will then veer right for a last chance to enter the Coastal Trail as it climbs to the chalet.) Then turn right at a "T."

Mi. 4.7 Turn right at the first turnoff to take Arlene's back to Mize Loop. (If you started the loop from the Coastal Trail, continue straight here and ride to the next intersection. There you'll see a directional sign. This is mile 0.8 of the ride description. Ride to the gravel trail and turn right following the directions from here.)

Mi. 4.8 Go right, then continue straight on the Ski for Women Cutoff.

Mi. 5.1 Reenter the Mize Loop at mile 0.8 of that route, turning right to return to the Stadium.

Lekisch Trail

The Lekisch Trail can be accessed from the Stadium as well as from the Kincaid Hills section of the park or the paved Tony Knowles Coastal Trail. Most riders find this to be one of the most challenging routes in the park because of the quick transitions from steep descents to steep climbs. It also can be confusing for those not using a map because of the frequent intersections along the way, but new maps installed at some intersections are helpful.

3-11 Lekisch Trail

Difficulty: Moderate to difficult. Steep hills and loose sand on hills and corners.

Surface: Midwidth mostly grass surface with some sand. Late summer has a singletrack feel with a narrow dirt line going through tall grass.

Distance: 4.4-mile loop.

The Andrew Lekisch Trail System is a series of interconnected loops with one climb and descent after another. Riders new to the route will check their maps frequently as they make their way through the series of short, challenging loops. Sandy sections can make it difficult to get traction or control your bicycle. It is considered a more difficult trail partially for this reason. As challenging as it is, the route also features a 360-degree view of the Anchorage Bowl and surrounding area.

This description will follow the longest route, known as the 7.5 Kilometer Loop. Park at the Stadium lot and ride down to the Stadium, heading left toward the Lekisch Tunnel at the south end. Mileage begins at the tunnel entrance.

Mi. 0.0 Ride through the tunnel and arrive at a display of flowers and ferns in this memorial garden. Turn left and follow the sign directing you to "Andrew's Trail." Climb and stay to the right where the trail forks. (Left takes you to Margaux's.) Follow the signs for the 7.5 Km route.

Mi. 0.3 Keep right as a connector trail to the left leads to the top of Hair Pin, Route 3-7. Turn left at the next junction. (A right returns to the tunnel.) The trail loops

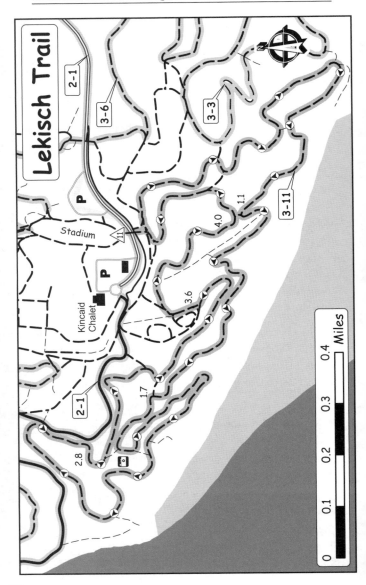

around, climbing and descending on trails that vary from grassy to sandy.

Mi. 0.9 Approach a sandy right curve and descend with caution.

Mi. 1.1 Stay left for the 7.5 Km Loop. (A right here will take you back to the tunnel.)

Mi. 1.5 An overlook above the biathlon range gives you a view over the chalet. The trail curves left and descends.

Mi. 1.7 At a "T" at the top of a climb, go left to stay on the 7.5 Km Loop. (A right turn goes to the biathlon range.)

Mi. 1.9 Veer left. A second overlook on the right offers views of the water below and Fire Island about four miles in the distance. Use caution on the left-turning descent, which may have loose sand.

Mi. 2.5 A descent takes you to the loop, off the bluff.

Mi. 2.6 The trail levels off as mature birch trees in the more open area. Soon the trail will climb again.

Mi. 2.8 Veer right to stay on the dirt trail. (A sign points to the Tony Knowles Coastal Trail. A few more small connectors also lead to the paved route.)

Mi. 3.0 At the top of a climb, the Coastal Trail comes into view to the left before you descend.

Mi. 3.3 Veer right as another left leads to the Coastal Trail. Then turn left at a "T" and continue to climb. A few false summits tease before you reach the top of the climb at mile 3.5. Descend once again.

Mi. 3.6   Arrive at a paved trail and go right, past the biathlon markers. Follow the pavement past a light pole.

Mi. 3.7   Turn right into a sandy area, and leave the pavement just before a disc golf goal basket. Stay right of a trail map sign to begin the final section of the ride. The trail climbs, then curves left at a gravely section.

Mi. 4.0   Turn left at this intersection. (A right here returns you to mile 1.1 of the ride.)

Mi. 4.1   Stay left at the bottom of a hill.

Mi. 4.3   Veer right and continue to descend, arriving at the memorial flower display. Turn left to ride through the tunnel.

Mi. 4.4   The ride ends on the Stadium side of the tunnel.

Chapter 4

Far North Bicentennial Park and Campbell Tract

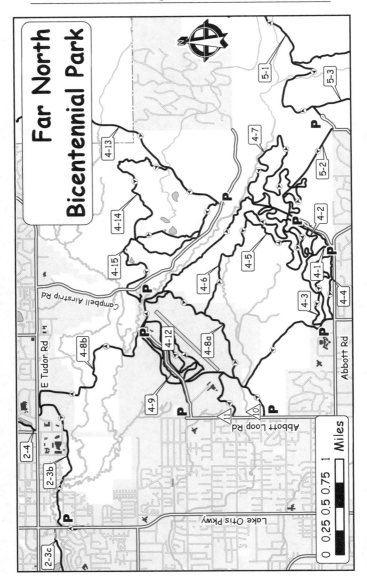

Far North Bicentennial Park

The beauty of Far North Bicentennial Park and the neighboring Campbell Tract on Anchorage's east side is in the diversity of trails and mountain scenery. Wide ski trails, obstacles and several miles of singletrack will challenge beginning and intermediate riders. The area also has sustained climbs and fast descents, especially when linked with the Chugach State Park trails.

FNBP is a municipal park of over 2,600 acres, while the Campbell Tract's 730 acres are managed by the Bureau of Land Management. Because land managers work together on trail issues, riders experience a seamless transition from one land-owner to the other, often unaware of the moment that they cross from municipal to federal land or vice versa.

The trails are easily accessed from paved greenbelt trails and street-side bike paths in many neighborhoods, making the park popular with commuters and a variety of park users almost year-round.

Before venturing out on the trails in the spring, riders should be aware of areas that may be closed. Trails in FNBP are closed to bicycles during the muddy spring breakup until the official reopening, usually June 1. Closures on the Campbell Tract may be different, so it is best to check with officials before riding. (See Resources for more information.) This guide includes routes that are considered open and legal for bicycles. During the snowy winters, trails listed as multi-use are open to cyclists and other users. See Chapter Eight, Winter Bicycling, for more information.

Hillside ski trails are mostly wide and can be loose and rocky in some places. Narrower multi-use trails like Rover's Run, Black Bear and Moose Meadow offer a more rustic, intimate feel. The section of the park north of Campbell Airstrip Road has some technical singletracks, some passing through trees spaced just wide enough to fit a handlebar.

Heavy use has led to erosion on a few trails. Exposed roots and standing water may be encountered even days after a rain. On narrower trails, riders should not ride around these mud holes because that will only make them wider. Instead, slow down to ride through them or choose a less muddy route. If a trail is listed as open, it's up to each rider to decide whether to ride it.

You can expect to see a great variety of wildlife in the park, including moose, bear, lynx and hares. Many birds can be spotted as well, including ruby-crowned kinglets and hermit thrush in summer. In winter, the common raven is a familiar sight. You may also spot gray jays and even bald eagles. Salmon in Campbell Creek attract bears that live in the park. You may see black or brown (grizzly) bears in any part of the park, so take time to learn about bear behavior and how to avoid dangerous encounters.

Major Trailheads

Far North Bicentennial Park/Campbell Tract can be accessed from several trailheads. Some have gates that are locked late in the day, so make note of this before parking at any trailhead.

Access from the South

Hillside Trailhead

The Hillside trailhead is on the south end of the park on Abbott Road. From the Seward Highway, take Dimond Boulevard east, toward the mountains. The road curves and becomes Abbott Road, then crosses Lake Otis Parkway followed by Abbott Loop Road, with stoplights at each intersection. Just after Service High School, at mile 3.8, turn left into the Hillside parking lot and park at the trailhead. (If the road begins curving to the right, you've gone too far.) If you want to park at Hilltop Ski Area, pass through a gate on the east end of the parking lot. The gate to Hilltop is normally open daily from 7:45 a.m. until 11 p.m., so make note of the time before parking there. You may wish to park at Service High School for some routes, but you should only do so when school is not in session.

Access from the West

Abbott Loop Community Park Trailhead

This park-within-a-park was established to provide ball fields for Little League teams. The expanded trailhead has parking for dozens of vehicles. Located on Abbott Loop Road, between Abbott Road and East 68th Avenue, the trailhead offers easy access to the Hillside trails as well as the trails of the Campbell Tract. The parking lot will have a gate that is locked nightly. Be sure to check the times before parking there.

From the Seward Highway, take Dimond Boulevard east, toward the mountains. The road curves and becomes Abbott Road, then crosses Lake Otis Parkway. At mile 2.1, turn left onto Abbott Loop Road. At mile 2.7, turn right into the trailhead parking lot.

Lore Road Trailhead

This BLM trailhead is best for those biking to the trails and is popular with equestrians. The unmarked entrance is just northeast of the intersection of Abbott Loop and Lore roads. Traveling north on Abbott Loop Road, pass the Abbott Loop Community Park trailhead. Go past a horse stable on the left and arrive at the Lore Road intersection. Just past this intersection, park in a gravel pullout on the right. (It's just 0.3 mile north of the Community Park trailhead.) The trail begins on the other side of the bushes with a short descent.

Smokejumper Trailhead

Smokejumper is a small but popular trailhead on BLM land. From the north, take Lake Otis Parkway to 68th Avenue and turn left. (Bike lanes on both sides of 68th and a separated bike path on the south side of the street make this a good commuting route.) About one mile from Lake Otis, 68th ends at Abbott Loop Road. Turn right, then make an immediate left toward the BLM and the Campbell Creek Science Center. The Smokejumper trailhead is ahead on the left, just before a split in the road. Take Moose Track Trail or ride the Science Center road (to the left after the trailhead) into the park.

Campbell Creek Science Center

Beyond the Smokejumper trailhead is the gate to the Campbell Creek Science Center road. It is locked nightly at 5 p.m., but it may be open after hours for events or meetings. Signs at the gate and in the parking lot list the closing time for that day. It is normally closed on federal holidays and weekends. While you may use the Science Center parking lot, Smokejumper is a better choice. No parking is allowed along the Science Center road.

Access from the North

Campbell Airstrip Trailhead (Formerly Known as Buckner and Often Referred to as the Mile 1.1 Trailhead)

From Lake Otis Parkway, go east (toward the mountains) on Tudor Road. After 2.5 miles, turn right at the stoplight at the intersection of Tudor and Campbell Airstrip Road. (Baxter Road is to the left.) You'll see a sign for the Alaska Botanical Gardens. Just before the 1-mile point on Campbell Airstrip Road, cross a bridge over North Fork of Campbell Creek, then a mushing tunnel. The trailhead is on the right. The trailhead is easy to get to by bicycle and parts of the route include bike paths that are separated from the road.

North and South Bivouac

This pair of trailheads is 2.3 miles up Campbell Airstrip road from the intersection with Tudor. North is on the left; South on the right. North Bivouac is sometimes referred to as the Tank Trail trailhead. South Bivouac is sometimes referred to as the Spencer Loop trailhead.

Hillside, Besh and Service Loops

These Hillside trails were designed as a series of inter-connected ski loops. They use the rolling terrain and give your legs a good workout whether on skis or bike. The trails have many intersections, and the correct route isn't always obvious to riders who are new to the park. Link them together for a good warmup to other trails.

4-1 Hillside Loop

Difficulty: Easy to moderate with some steep hills.

Surface: Wide, gravel surface.

Winter: No.

Distance: 1.5-mile loop.

This ride begins at the Hillside trailhead.

Mi. 0.0 Start at the information sign and turn right to climb the hill away from the parking lot. Continue straight as a new route merges from the left. (This is the end of a bypass that allows riders and skiers who are doing laps to travel the Hillside Loop without passing the busy trailhead each time.)

Mi. 0.2 Stay left to ride the Hillside Loop. (A right will take you onto the Besh Loop and to intersections with Spencer and Richter loops.)

Mi. 0.3 Stay straight. (A right turn would take you to the end of the Besh Loop.)

Mi. 0.4 Continue straight. (Coaches' Cutoff is to the left. If you take this shortcut, in less than a tenth of a mile, you'll arrive at mile 1.3 of the Hillside Loop.)

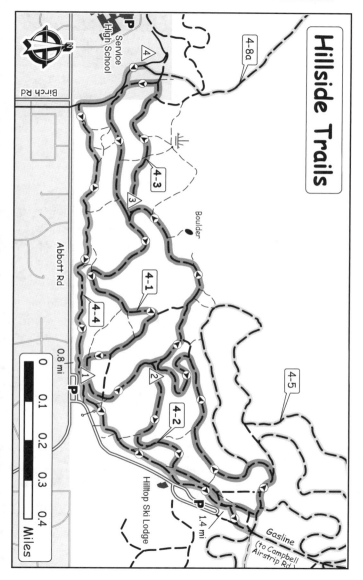

Hillside Trails

Option

A few smaller, singletrack trails leave Hillside Loop to the right. For a side trip, at mile 0.6, turn right on a singletrack. (Light pole 25 is across from the singletrack.) Just down the trail, you'll see a glacial erratic, a large boulder left by a receding glacier. This is the easiest entrance to the geologic landmark.

To continue on the Hillside Loop, stay on the main trail.

Mi. 0.7 Continue straight, on the main route. A trail branching off to the right may pique your curiosity, but it's called the Bog Trail for a good reason. It may be dry at the outset, but eventually, even during the driest summers, you'll end up in the dark muddy soil for part of this quarter-mile route.

Mi. 0.8 This spacious four-way intersection is known as Conversation Corner. Stay to the far left to continue on the Hillside Loop, or veer right to take the Service Loop and reach the Tour of Anchorage route.

Mi. 1.1 A bench welcomes you to the top of a hill. This is a good place to take a break and enjoy the view to the west.

Mi. 1.2 Keep on the main route to ride the entire Hillside Loop.

Option

At mile 1.2, a short (0.2 mile) singletrack to the right follows a ridge of low-growing trees then reconnects with the Hillside Loop at mile 1.5, just before the end of the loop.

Mi. 1.3 After descending and coasting up a short hill, to the left you'll see the end of Coaches' Cutoff. Go right to continue the loop.

Mi. 1.4 A split in the trail gives you two options: go right and descend to return to the trailhead, or turn left to finish the loop and continue on more trails.

Mi. 1.5 If you turned right, you'll finish at the trailhead information sign.

Mi. 1.5 If you turned left, you'll veer left here as riders from the trailhead merge from the right.

Mi. 1.7 Arrive at the intersection with Besh Loop.

4-2 Besh Loop

Difficulty: Easy.

Surface: Wide gravel.

Winter: No.

Distance: 1.5-mile loop.

A number of alternate routes branch away from the Besh Loop, especially as you near Hilltop and intersections with Spencer Loop and the Gasline Multi-Use Corridor. It's easy to take a wrong turn, so this description will point out the major obvious turns.

The ride begins where Besh intersects with Hillside Loop.

Mi. 0.0 Go right on a descent.

Mi. 0.3 Stay right. (Ann's Alley veers left, cutting out almost half of the route, before reconnecting with Besh at mile 1.0. Turn left to continue after riding this shortcut.)

Mi. 0.4 A sign alerts you to a busy area ahead. Descend from here.

Mi. 0.5 Stay on the center route as you pass Eagle Bypass on the left and the Hilltop parking area on the right. Veer left.

Mi. 0.6 Go straight. (Right goes to Spencer Loop and the Gasline Multi-Use Corridor.) Then turn left at the "T" and climb past the Double Bubble on the right and Eagle Bypass on the left.

Mi. 0.7 Veer left to stay on Besh. (Ridge and Richter trails drop away to the right.)

Mi. 0.8 Stay straight, passing the end of Richter Loop on the right.)

Mi. 1.0 Continue straight as Ann's Alley enters from the left.

Mi. 1.2 Stay left as the trail splits. (If you go straight, you'll quickly intersect with mile 0.3 of Hillside Loop.)

Mi. 1.4 Stay right and climb. (Left takes you on another lap on the Besh Loop or to other trails mentioned above.)

Mi. 1.5 Besh ends as you intersect with the Hillside Loop. Turn right to ride Hillside (Route 4-1).

4-3 Service Loop

Difficulty: Easy.

Surface: Wide gravel.

Winter: No.

Distance: 0.8-mile loop.

The Service Loop connects Hillside to Service High School and the Tour of Anchorage route, which takes you toward the BLM Campbell Tract trails. This ride starts at Conversation Corner, where the Hillside and Service loops meet.

Mi. 0.0   Start on the outbound route and note light pole 21 on the left side of the trail.

Mi. 0.3   Stay left at a "Y" in the trail. This is the Why Stop junction. (If you veer right here and stay on the main trail, at just over a tenth of a mile you'll reach a four-way intersection. The Tour of Anchorage route, or Homestead Trail, is to the right. Straight is Randy's Loop, which runs behind Service High; left takes you to the southern end of the Tour of Anchorage route.)

Having gone left at Why Stop, turn left at the next intersection. (Go straight, then right to reach the Tour of Anchorage route.)

Mi. 0.4   Continue on Service Loop until you arrive at an intersection with a paved trail running east-west and a sports field immediately in front of you. Stay left, on the dirt trail, and climb. (If you turn right on the paved path, you'll arrive at Service High School. Left on the pavement leads to the Abbott Multi-Use Trail, Route 4-4, which parallels Abbott Road or to a bridge that crosses the road.)

Mi. 0.8   Arrive once again at Conversation Corner and the intersection with Hillside Loop. Take the rightmost option for the Hillside Loop. Take a hard left to ride the Service Loop again or to take it to the Tour of Anchorage route.

Multi-Use Link

The Abbott Multi-Use Trail provides a link for riders making their way from the Hillside trailhead to the Homestead Trail and other multi-use routes in FNBP. This is especially important in winter when ski trails are off-limits to all other users. In the summer, the route is a shortcut for those not wishing to take the more twisty trails to reach Homestead Trail. A continuation of the Abbott Multi-Use Trail is the Gasline Multi-Use Corridor, which links riders to Rover's Run and the South Bivouac trailhead.

4-4 Abbott Multi-Use Trail

Difficulty: Easy to moderate with some hills.

Surface: Midwidth dirt and rock surface, can be bumpy.

Winter: Yes.

Distance: 1.5 miles one way (2.4 miles one way to reach the South Bivouac trailhead).

While this route is available to ride almost year-round, the Abbott Multi-Use Trail is most appreciated for providing a much-needed link for winter trail users, particularly those who aren't allowed on the ski-only routes. Cyclists, equestrians, skijorers and walkers share this route, which links the Tour of Anchorage with the Gasline Multi-Use Corridor, just north of Hilltop. You may notice multiple singletrack connector trails entering on both sides of the trail throughout this route. Because they connect with ski-only routes, it's best to explore them during the summer.

This description starts where the Tour of Anchorage route meets the paved bike path that runs between Service

High and Abbott Road. You can also easily access it from the Hillside trailhead or the Gasline route.

Mi. 0.0   Ride east (toward the mountains). The paved path will climb gradually. You'll see large painted stars on the ground along the side of the trail, then approach a metal bridge.

Mi. 0.2   Just before you reach the metal bridge, turn left onto the dirt trail. Some benches along the trail offer places to relax.

Mi. 0.8   Pass an orange skijoring sign. Go straight at this intersection to stay on the multi-use trail and reach the Hillside trailhead.

Option

In summer, turn left at the 0.8-mile point and arrive at mile 1.5 of the Hillside Loop. Just as you arrive at Hillside Loop, look over your left shoulder to see a singletrack. That trail leads to mile 1.2 of Hillside Loop and is worth a spin.

Mi. 0.9   Arrive at a wooden sign post just west of the Hillside trailhead parking area.

To continue on a multi-use route, ride east (toward the mountains) on a mostly gravel route, behind the trailhead sign, toward another sign-post that is labeled "multi use corridor." In winter, don't enter the ski trails, which are to the left. The trail enters the woods and climbs.

Mi. 1.0   Stay left at an orange skijoring sign and climb.

Mi. 1.3   Stay right on the main route and descend toward Hilltop Ski Area. The trail then levels off.

Mi. 1.4   Arrive at a wide area where multi-use and ski trails meet. To the right is Hilltop parking. Go straight, noting light post 201 on the left.

Mi. 1.5   Turn right to continue on a narrow multi-use route. Veer left onto the Gasline portion of the multi-use corridor and continue straight to arrive at the trail sign that marks the entrance to Spencer Loop, just before the 1.6-mile point.

Continue to the South Bivouac trailhead on Campbell Airstrip Road.

Mi. 1.6   Ride north on the wide Gasline Multi-Use Corridor, past a trail intersection.

Mi. 1.9   Arrive at a trail junction. Ride past the first right turn, which goes to Spencer Loop. Immediately after that turn, the next right continues the multi-use route. Turn right here and descend. (If you went straight instead of turning, you'd ride a steep descent and arrive at the Campbell Creek. From here, you could go left for Rover's Run, right to rejoin the multi-use route or straight to cross a small bridge and climb a steep rocky hill to the parking lot.)

Mi. 2.1   Pass the entrance to Rover's Run on the left.

Mi. 2.2   Go straight to cross the Campbell Creek on a bridge. (Right is Spencer Loop.) Take the right fork where the trail splits to ride the uphill route (left is the downhill route).

Mi. 2.4   Arrive at the South Bivouac trailhead.

Option

An alternative to staying on the multi-use trail is to cross the Hillside parking lot and turn left to ride the road to Hilltop Ski Area. You can enter the trails here.

Narrower Routes

Some routes in Far North Bicentennial Park remain narrower than the upgraded ski trails like the Hillside and Besh loops. They offer more rustic settings with trees closer to the trails and a more natural riding surface. The roots and rocks make for some challenging terrain, but it's also a pleasant ride for cyclists seeking a more intimate trail experience.

4-5 Richter and Ridge Loops

Difficulty: Moderate to difficult with steep hills.

Surface: Midwidth route with grass and dirt surface; can be rooty.

Winter: No.

Distance: 2.6-mile loop.

These trails take off from the Besh Loop (Route 4-2), just after the intersection with Besh and the Double Bubble portion of the Spencer Loop (Route 4-8). The ride mileage starts at the intersection where the Gasline Multi-Use Corridor meets the end of Spencer Loop.

Mi. 0.0 From the sign at the junction of Spencer Loop and the Gasline, go west (left when facing the map sign), riding past the Double Bubble on your right. Climb to the top of a hill where you'll see a sign for the Richter and Ridge loop trails.

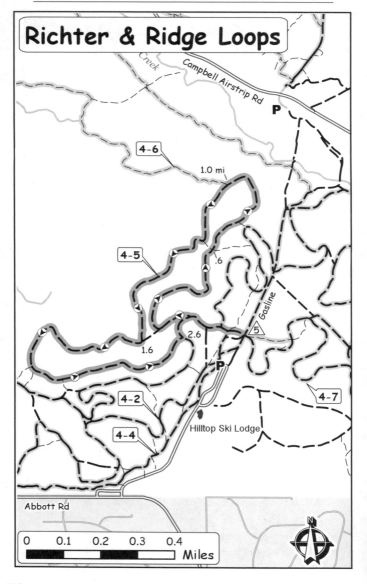

Richter & Ridge Loops

Campbell Airstrip Rd

Creek

P

4-6

1.0 mi

4-5

.6

Gasline

5

1.6

2.6

P

4-2

4-7

Hilltop Ski Lodge

4-4

Abbott Rd

| 0 | 0.1 | 0.2 | 0.3 | 0.4 |

Miles

N

Mi. 0.1 Turn right to descend onto Richter Loop. (If you are riding only Richter Loop, go straight as you descend.) Make a sweeping right turn part way down the hill to ride the Ridge Loop.

Mi. 0.6 Stay on the main route as you pass a single-track shortcut. Continue along the main trail until you reach a steep, fast descent.

Mi. 1.0 Continue straight to stay on the Ridge Loop. (Right is Black Bear Trail, which leads to Moose Meadow and other routes on the Campbell Tract. See Route 4-6.)

Mi. 1.6 Arrive at a "T" where the sign reads, "End Ridge Loop." Turn right to rejoin Richter Loop.

Mi. 2.6 Richter ends at Besh Loop after a steep climb. Turn right to continue on Besh, or go left to quickly return to the Gasline (be aware that you are riding against the majority of the traffic).

4-6 Rover's Run, Moose Meadow and Black Bear Trails

Difficulty: Moderate to difficult with steep hills, roots and rocks.

Surface: Singletrack and midwidth dirt and gravel surfaces, obstacles.

Winter: All three of these trails are open in winter, but the Ridge and Richter trails, which complete the loop, are not. For winter riding, link with the Tour of Anchorage and other multi-use routes.

Distance: 5.3-mile loop.

This loop ride takes you along some of the narrower

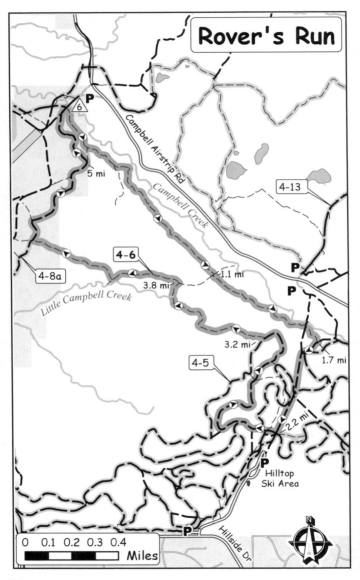

Rover's Run

trails in Far North Bicentennial Park and links the BLM and Hillside trails. Keep in mind that Rover's Run is slow to dry after a rain. Ride through, not around, the puddles, or choose a different route until the trail dries. This loop begins at the wooden bollards at the Campbell Airstrip trailhead.

Mi. 0.0   Ride across the bridge, then turn left onto the Viewpoint Trail.

Mi. 0.2   Turn left onto Rover's Run.

Mi. 1.1   Stay on Rover's as Moose Meadow Trail intersects from the right. The South Fork of Campbell Creek is on the left.

Mi. 1.6   Arrive at a meadow. Go straight into the woods to intersect the Gasline. (A steep gravel hill to the right of the meadow provides a challenging alternative route to the Gasline Multi-Use Corridor. Left of the meadow, a narrow bridge crosses the creek. Ride up the steep gravel hill and turn left to reach the South Bivouac trailhead.)

Mi. 1.7   Turn right onto the Gasline and climb, veering left at the top of the hill. Ride south toward the Hilltop Ski Area on the Gasline Multi-Use Corridor.

Mi. 2.2   Turn right at a sign with a map and information about the Nordic Skiing Association of Anchorage (NSAA). Pass the intersection to the Double Bubble of Spencer Loop on the right, then a trail entering from the left. Keep climbing to arrive at a sign for the Richter and Ridge loops.

Mi. 2.4   Veer right to descend onto Richter, then make a sweeping right turn onto Ridge. A few steep climbs and descents take you to the intersection labeled "Campbell Airstrip Trails."

Mi. 3.2 This is the Black Bear Trail. Turn right to ride the route which is mostly a singletrack descent. Remember to yield to those who are climbing.

Mi. 3.8 After crossing a small plank bridge, arrive at Moose Meadow and turn left.

Mi. 4.5 Turn right onto the Viewpoint Trail.

Mi. 5.0 Turn left to climb Birch Knob. Make a descent as the trail veers right.

Mi. 5.3 Arrive at the bridge over the Campbell Creek. Cross the bridge for the Airstrip trailhead.

Option

While on Ridge Loop, at mile 2.8 of the route turn left onto a singletrack and follow a twisty trail for less than a tenth of a mile. Turn right to rejoin Ridge Loop and climb gently toward Black Bear Trail, which will be just after the 3.0-mile point. Turn left onto Black Bear to continue the ride, adjusting your mileage accordingly.

Spencer Loop

Spencer Loop climbs to the east above the Gasline Multi-Use Corridor. It also includes a section of trail on the west side of the corridor. Its climbs challenge riders, especially early in the season, but the scenic views paired with the thrills of the descents make the suffering worthwhile.

4-7 Spencer Loop, Including Double Bubble

Difficulty: Moderate to difficult with steep, long climbs and twisting descents.

Surface: Wide with gravel and grass.

Winter: No.

Distance: 4.9-mile loop.

Spencer Loop is the Hillside trail by which many riders and skiers measure their season's performance. It has longer, more sustained climbs than most of the city's trails. For those wanting to get off their bikes for a short walk, it offers a look at a gorge on the South Fork of Campbell Creek and spectacular views of Anchorage and Cook Inlet.

The trail surface drains well overall, with the wettest areas being where the trail abuts the Hilltop Ski Area, especially in the late spring just as the trails are opening for the summer biking season.

Spencer Loop is intersected by the Upper Gasline Trail. For a challenging hill climb, you can ride up this trail to Prospect Heights and on to the Powerline Trail. Just beware that riders fly pretty fast down this trail in the opposite direction!

This route starts with the Double Bubble part of the trail, then crosses the Gasline Multi-Use Corridor. It begins at the NSAA information sign just north of the Hilltop parking lot. If you park at Hilltop, remember that the lot is gated, so note the closing time before beginning the ride.

Mi. 0.0 Start at the NSAA information sign. (This is also where the ride ends.) Ride west and take the first right where a sign marks the entrance to the Double Bubble. The trail will climb and descend the first stretch of trail as it loops around.

Mi. 0.3 At the bottom of the hill you may notice a small walking path into the woods on the right side of the trail leading to a couple boulders left by a receding glacier. It makes an interesting side trip for curious riders and those interested in the geology of the Anchorage area.

Mi. 0.4 The trail comes very close to the Gasline Multi-Use Corridor, but stay left on the main trail for more of the route.

Mi. 0.8 Cross the Gasline, then veer left into the woods and begin another climb.

Mi. 1.0 Stay straight on the main route as you pass the Bear Cut Off on your right. (This is a shortcut if you want to climb to the Upper Gasline Trail into the Chugach State Park.) Descend on the steepest part of the trail, a curving route with loose gravel.

Mi. 1.2 Keep right. (Left goes to the Gasline Multi-Use Corridor.)

Mi. 1.3 Keep right. (Left goes to the South Bivouac trailhead.) The trail swings close to the South Fork of Campbell Creek. Pace yourself as you begin a series of climbs. A sign announcing "Wall Street" means you're almost to the top.

Mi. 2.2 The trail bends to the right before making the final climb to the top.

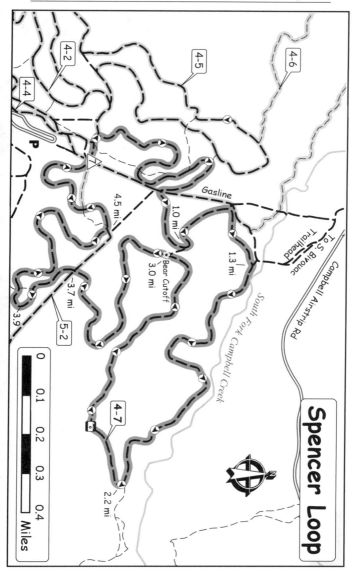

Spencer Loop

Option

Notice a narrow trail at mile 2.2, on the outside of the corner (left side). This route is considered by Chugach State Park (at the other trail entrance) to be an illegal connector between the two parks. However, the municipality considers it a legal trail. So, while it's technically off-limits to biking at the top, it does make a good side trip on foot to look at the gorge carved by the South Fork of Campbell Creek.

Mi. 2.4 From the overlook at the top of the climb, begin a fast, twisting descent.

Mi. 3.0 Stay straight where the Bear Cut Off connector trail joins from the right.

Mi. 3.7 Arrive at a clearing and the intersection with the Upper Gasline Trail. Continue straight. (A left turn will take you up a steep rocky climb to Chugach State Park and Prospect Heights trailhead, Route 5-2. A shortcut to the right takes you almost to the end of Spencer Loop as it descends straight, then veers left back into the woods and onto the main trail, turning right.

Mi. 3.9 Continue straight. (A trail to the left going into the woods is the lower entrance to the Llama Trail. It is considered by the municipality to be a woodland trail, not a biking route. The trail isn't marked, and many bikers have adopted it as a less-steep, yet technical, connector to the Prospect Heights trailhead.)

To complete Spencer Loop, continue on a series of descents and small climbs. You'll swing close to Hilltop two more times. During spring riding these are usually the muddiest parts of the trail as the packed snow takes a while to melt. Watch the final corners and be aware of possible ruts on the last section of trail.

Mi. 4.5 Stay straight on the main route as a trail enters from the right. This route is popular with riders descending from Upper Gasline. Slow as you enter the busy area where Spencer crosses the Gasline Multi-Use Corridor at the bottom of the hill.

Mi. 4.9 Arrive at the NSAA information sign where you started.

Option

Directions from the South Bivouac trailhead to the start of Spencer Loop

Mi. 0.0 Start at the wooden bollards at the South Bivouac trailhead and pass the information sign.

Mi. 0.1 Take the right fork where the trail splits. (Left is preferred as the uphill route.)

Mi. 0.2 Cross the bridge over the South Fork of Campbell Creek, then keep right to follow the trail. (Turning left here leads to mile 1.3 of the route.)

Mi. 0.3 Stay straight as you pass an intersection on your right that connects to Rover's Run. Climb to the top of the hill and veer left, toward the Hilltop Ski Area.

Mi. 0.8 A map posted on the right at the intersection is the ride starting point. (Spencer Loop exits the woods on the left, so this is also where the ride ends.)

Tour of Anchorage Route

The Tour of Anchorage is a late-winter ski race (up to 50 kilometers in distance) that starts at Service High School and crosses Anchorage, ending with a final climb to the Kincaid Park Stadium. It also is the nickname for a series of differently named trails that make up the portion of the race route that crosses Far North Bicentennial Park and Campbell Tract. The route can confuse people who aren't familiar with the multiple names. There are few signs, which can add to that confusion.

The route is typically wide and can have some puddles after a rain. In 2004, some sections were smoothed and gravel capped to eliminate the larger mud holes. Some sections of the route escaped the capping and have more puddles than the gravel stretches. The result is a wide, often fast route connecting Service High School and Tudor Road, though some parts of the trail near Tudor do have muddy or wet spots. Watch your speed on the route; without the whoop-de-dos and roots, it's easy to go faster than other trail users would prefer.

4-8a Tour of Anchorage: Homestead and Viewpoint Trails

Difficulty: Easy to moderate with one steep hill.

Surface: Wide gravel with some dirt.

Winter: Yes.

Distance: 5.8 miles round trip (10.2 miles round trip when combined with Route 4-8b.)

The Tour route starts behind Service High School and has several access points. This description begins near

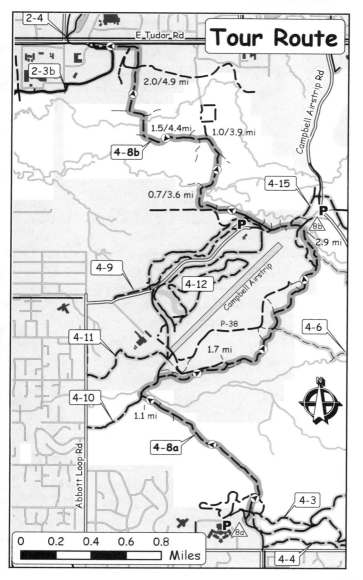

Tour Route

E. Tudor Rd

Campbell Airstrip Rd

2-4

2-3b

2.0/4.9 mi

1.5/4.4 mi   1.0/3.9 mi

4-8b

0.7/3.6 mi

4-15

P

8b

2.9 mi

4-9

4-12

Campbell Airstrip

P-38

4-6

4-11

1.7 mi

4-10

1.1 mi

4-8a

N

Abbott Loop Rd

4-3

P

8a

4-4

0   0.2   0.4   0.6   0.8

Miles

Service High, where the dirt Homestead Trail leaves the pavement. From the Hillside trailhead, take the Abbott Multi-Use Trail (Route 4-4) west 0.9 mile. Turn right onto the pavement (a bridge to the left crosses Abbott Road) and descend 0.2 mile, passing a service gate on the left and Service Loop on the right. A dirt multi-use trail turns right. This is the Homestead Trail.

Mi. 0.0 Ride away from the pavement and continue straight through two four-way intersections. After the second one, the trail begins to mostly descend toward the Campbell Tract.

Mi. 1.1 Arrive at a three-way intersection. Turn right to stay on the Tour route, now called Coyote Trail. (If you turn left and climb a hill, in just over 0.3 mile you'll arrive at a wide clearing with sports fields and the Abbott Loop Community Park trailhead. For people living in the Abbott Loop area, this is a good place to access the trails.) Cross a bridge and notice a bench on the left next to the creek.

Cross the boundary onto the Campbell Tract, BLM land. This section of trail can be muddy after a rain.

Mi. 1.2 Turn right onto Viewpoint Trail.

Mi. 1.3 Stay on the main route as you pass a trail on the left, the P-38 Lightning Trail.

Mi. 1.7 At a four-way intersection, turn right to descend. The trail is steep and the surface can be loose and gravely, so use care. (Straight ahead is where climbers will meet and rejoin the route. Left is an access road.

Note

Many people climb this route, but there's an alternative if you're coming from the other direction. When riding away from the Airstrip area, just before you reach the bottom of the hill, turn right at the signpost. An antenna is also to the right. Climb the uphill route and turn left to reach the four-way intersection. Go straight to continue. (From the Airstrip trailhead, the turn is just 1.1 miles up the trail.)

Continue riding as the trail levels off.

Mi. 2.1   Go straight as you pass Moose Meadow Trail.

Mi. 2.6   Go straight as you pass Rover's Run. Both Moose Meadow and Rover's Run trails offer alternate loop routes to return to the Hillside trails.

Mi. 2.8   Arrive at an information sign at a clearing.

Mi. 2.9   Continue straight using Route 4-8b to get to Tudor Road, or turn right to cross the bridge and arrive at the Campbell Airstrip trailhead.

Option: P-38 Lightning Trail

Difficulty:	Easy.
Surface:	Mostly gravel doubletrack.
Winter:	No.
Distance:	2.8 round trip.

For an easier alternative to the Viewpoint Trail portion of the Tour of Anchorage, use the trail reclaimed by the BLM and volunteers in 2004. A summer route only, portions are open only to mushers during the winter. The trail name, P-38 Lightning, is a tribute to the Lockheed fighter planes that were stationed at the airstrip during World War II.

Mi. 0.0 Begin at the intersection of the Coyote and Viewpoint trails, riding northeast on Viewpoint. Crest a small knoll and veer left on the short descent onto the P-38 Trail.

Mi. 0.1 Cross an access road and continue straight.

Mi. 0.2 Continue straight as another trail joins from the left.

Mi. 0.7 Keep left to remain on the trail.

Mi. 1.0 At a "Y" in the trail go left. (Right will take you to the Viewpoint Trail in 0.1 mile, where you can take a left and arrive at the bridge at the Airstrip trailhead after just over 0.3 mile).

Mi. 1.2 Veer right, away from the sign that announces that you are near the runway, into a more wooded area.

Mi. 1.3 Arrive at Birch Knob Trail and turn left. The trail then veers right toward the bridge.

Mi. 1.4 Intersect the Viewpoint Trail at the bridge.

4-8b Tour of Anchorage: Old Rondy Trail

Difficulty: Easy to moderate with some rough, slippery sections after rain.

Surface: Wide gravel with dirt portions; two wooden bridges might have loose boards.

Winter: Yes.

Distance: 4.4 miles round trip.

This route picks up where the Route 4-8a description from Homestead Trail to Viewpoint Trail left off. Follow signs for "Tour of Anchorage" or "Old Rondy Trail"; the names can be used interchangeably for this portion of the route. Mileage begins where Viewpoint meets the bridge, across the creek from the Campbell Airstrip trailhead.

Mi. 0.0 Ride west on Old Rondy Trail and cross a mushing trail.

Mi. 0.1 At a three-way intersection, veer right, noting a sign for Old Rondy Trail. (Left is the most direct route to the Campbell Creek Science Center.)

Mi. 0.3 Continue straight as Moose Track Trail enters from the left. (Moose Track will take you toward the Science Center. A nature trail to the right follows the creek upstream. Watch for kids on the trails in this area, especially during summer weekdays.)

Mi. 0.5 Ride past a pullout on the left. Soon the gravel portion of the trail will end and the surface will become more natural and often wet.

Mi. 0.7 Arrive at a bridge over the South Fork of Campbell Creek. Watch for salmon in the stream during mid- to late summer and for brown and black bears looking for the salmon.

Mi. 0.9 The main trail curves to the left. (A second, abandoned, trail goes right and is often unnoticed when traveling in this direction.)

Mi. 1.0 Veer left at a fork and ride down a hill. On the left side of the trail, notice an old marker reading, "ski trail." An arrow points left. During the summer, a faint singletrack may be visible, while in winter the route remains ungroomed.

Mi. 1.3 Notice beaver activity along the trail and a pond on the left.

Mi. 1.5 A bridge crosses the North Fork of Campbell Creek.

Mi. 1.9 Arrive at an intersection with a dog mushing trail. During the winter, use caution and yield to mushers. The trail soon follows a fence next to an electrical substation.

Mi. 2.0 Ride around a red gate and turn left at a "T," riding west, parallel to Tudor Road. (This section of trail from the gate west can also have standing water and ruts.)

Mi. 2.2 Enter a paved path, the end of the trail.

An information sign is to your left. Go left to take the Campbell Creek trail (Route 2-3b), or go straight, then right to the Tudor Road street-side trail. A left from there takes you onto the bridge across Tudor. Cross the bridge and ride through a tunnel to get to University Lake and the APU trail system, routes 2-4 and 2-5.

Option

To get to the Old Rondy Trail from the Campbell Creek Science Center parking lot, go to the northeast corner of the lot. You'll see a trail going into the woods. This is the east end of Moose Track Trail. Go straight on it as it crosses a mushing trail. The next intersection is Old Rondy. Turn right to get to Viewpoint and the Hillside trails. Turn left to take Old Rondy to Tudor Road.

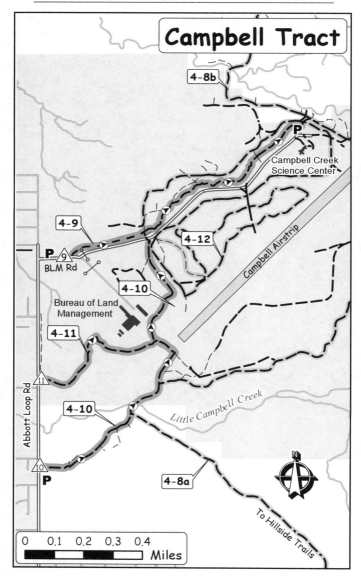

Campbell Tract

4-8b

Campbell Creek
Science Center

4-9

4-12

P
9
BLM Rd

4-10

Bureau of Land
Management

4-11

11

Campbell Airstrip

4-10

Little Campbell Creek

10

P

4-8a

To Hillside Trails

N

0   0.1   0.2   0.3   0.4

Miles

Campbell Tract

Several routes take riders into the Campbell Tract, allowing them to connect with the trails of FNBP. The more popular ones, Moose Track and Coyote Trail, have trailheads where visitors can park. A third route, the Lore Road Trail, is not as well known partially because its trailhead is hidden and has little parking. The three routes are all multi-use. A fourth route on the tract is for summer riding only; Balto Loop uses portions of some mushing trails for a fun singletrack ride. It is closed to bikes in the winter.

4-9 Moose Track Trail

Difficulty: Easy.

Surface: Midwidth, gravel surface.

Winter: Yes.

Distance: 2-mile round trip.

Moose Track is on the northwest side of the Campbell Tract and runs near the north side of the Science Center road. It has been modified to meet Americans with Disabilities Act standards so it is wheelchair accessible. Watch for some abrupt corners and trees close to the trail. This description starts at the Smokejumper trailhead, from which you can ride Moose Track Trail to reach the Campbell Creek Science Center or other trails.

Mi. 0.0 From the trailhead, ride into the woods and to the right.

Mi. 0.2 Continue straight. (On the right, a turnoff takes you to the Science Center road and to the Coyote Trail.)

Mi. 0.4   Pass a gravel storage area to your right.

Mi. 0.8   Continue straight. (Go right to exit the trail and connect with the road.)

Mi. 1.0   Arrive at an intersection. Turn left to take Moose Track several yards to the Old Rondy Trail; turn right to reach the Science Center.

4-10   Coyote Trail

Difficulty: Easy.

Surface: Mostly wide gravel and dirt surface.

Winter: Yes.

Distance: 2.2-mile round trip.

Coyote Trail provides a direct route to the park for those entering from Abbott Loop Road. Although primarily on BLM land, the Coyote Trail begins in Far North Bicentennial Park at the Abbott Loop Community Park trailhead.

Mi. 0.0   From the large boulders in the parking area, ride east (toward the mountains) into the woods and descend.

Mi. 0.3   Veer left where the route intersects the Homestead Trail, Route 4-8a. (Right leads to the Hillside trails.) Cross a bridge and continue straight.

Mi. 0.5   Stay straight as the Viewpoint Trail intersects from the right.

Mi. 0.7   The Lore Road Trail enters from the left. Continue straight, crossing the airstrip taxiway.

Mi. 1.1   Pass through an opening in a wooden rail

fence and arrive at the Science Center road. (Across the road is Moose Track Trail.) Turn left to reach Abbott Loop Road; go right to reach the Science Center and other trails.

4-11   Lore Road Trail

Difficulty: Easy to moderate.

Surface: Wide, doubletrack and singletrack tread with gravel and dirt; some roots.

Winter: Yes.

Distance: 1-mile round trip.

The Lore Road Trail offers another access point for riders in the Abbott Loop area. It's best to ride to the trailhead because of the limited amount of parking. Equestrians often use the Lore Road Trail to access other park trails. As always, you should watch your speed and yield to the horses. The description begins at the Lore Road trailhead.

Mi. 0.0   Look for an entry point that descends, then jogs right.

Mi. 0.2   Keep right as the trail curves at a junction, then gets wider.

Mi. 0.3   A sign marks the right turn into the woods. Ride the curvy singletrack to where it meets the Coyote Trail.

Mi. 0.5   At the Coyote Trail, turn right for Viewpoint Trail or to reach the Hillside trails; go left for the Science Center or the Old Rondy Trail headed for Tudor Road.

4-12 Balto Loop*

Difficulty: Moderate to difficult with roots and ruts. Most of route is quite level.

Surface: Mostly singletrack with some slightly wider tread.

Winter: No.

Distance: 3.6-mile loop.

*Balto Loop is a name chosen for the route by the author.

A number of mushing trails make their way through the Campbell Tract. While off-limits in the winter, during the summer months some of these trails offer singletrack riding for those looking for different scenery. This route covers parts of the 8, 12, and 16 Mile loops, the 1.4 Mile Loop and the Woodard Trail. It also uses a small part of the Coyote Trail. For simplicity, the route will be called Balto Loop.

The Balto Loop covers almost four miles of twisting trails and is intersected by several smaller trails. A wrong turn can have you wandering through this small area for some time. A cycle computer is helpful.

The mileage for this ride begins where Balto Loop crosses Science Center Way. You can access the loop from the Old Rondy (Tour of Anchorage) Trail or the Science Center road. From the Campbell Airstrip trailhead, ride west on the Old Rondy Trail. Turn left where Old Rondy meets Science Center Way and look for a sign showing a mushing sled, just after mile 0.2. Turn left to begin the ride. To access the route from the Science Center parking

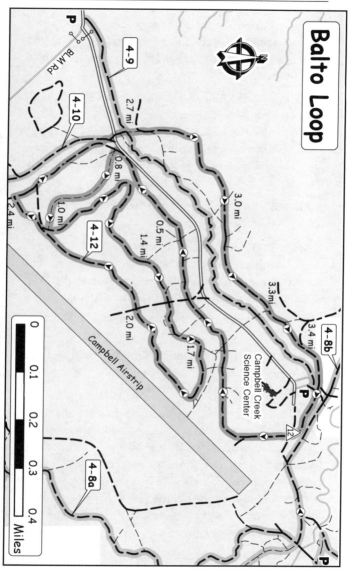

Balto Loop

BLM Rd

P

4-9

2.7 mi

4-10

0.8 mi

1.0 mi

1.2.4 mi

3.0 mi

0.5 mi

4-12

1.4 mi

3.3 mi

3.4 mi

4-8b

2.0 mi

1.7 mi

Campbell Airstrip

Campbell Creek
Science Center

P

12

4-8a

P

0	0.1	0.2	0.3	0.4

Miles

lot, go east from the lot on Science Center Way, past a brown metal gate. Watch for the mushing sled sign, and turn right for the trail entrance, less than a tenth of a mile from the gate.

Mi. 0.0   Go south onto the mushing trail. The surface starts off with large river rocks but soon becomes a softer trail with some roots. Stay right at a fork in the trail, then remain on this route as small foot paths enter from each side. The trail gets rooty as it travels through the mostly spruce forest.

Mi. 0.2   Ride straight through three four-way intersections. More birch trees appear.

Mi. 0.3   The trail enters an open area where a berm to the right separates the rocky trail from a grassy field. The Science Center road is on the opposite side of the field. Cross a gravel doubletrack and continue straight where you see a small mushing trail sign. The trail climbs a small bank then narrows.

Mi. 0.5   Go right at a fork where a faint trail goes left. The right trail widens, then becomes more faint as you approach and ride parallel to the road.

Mi. 0.8   As you reach a wooden fence, the trail veers left, away from the road, and splits. Go left to climb. As you climb, take another left to reach a ridge. The terrain levels off as you traverse the spruce- and birch-covered ridge. A steep descent takes you off the ridge; you'll veer left at the bottom of the hill (the 1.0-mile point) and follow the route as it passes alongside the ridge. The trail tread here is mostly singletrack.

Mi. 1.4   Go right at a fork. (Left goes to mile 0.5 of

the loop.) Follow the singletrack as it climbs a knoll then descends to the doubletrack gravel area.

Mi. 1.5   Cross the doubletrack.

Mi. 1.6   Veer left at a wide junction. The trail will be wider and splits into two paths for a few yards.

Mi. 1.7   Turn right into the singletrack. (Straight is a more used-looking, slightly wider path.) Go right at a "T" onto a slightly wider, rooty section.

Mi. 1.8   The main trail curves right as a faint single-track enters from the left.

Mi. 2.0   Enter an open area and continue straight across the gravel doubletrack. To the right is the Science Center road; to the left is the Campbell Airstrip, an active airstrip that for safety reasons is off-limits.

Mi. 2.1   Take either option at a split that rejoins in just a few yards. (Most take the right option.)

Mi. 2.4   Arrive at an intersection and take a hairpin right turn. (Left goes to the airstrip.)

Mi. 2.5   Ride past an intersection on the right, then veer left at a split, riding through a meadow to reach the Coyote Trail. Turn right onto Coyote and cross the road. Enter a trail directly across the road; it leads to Moose Track Trail.

Mi. 2.7   Cross Moose Track and enter a singletrack that is just right of a wooden trail sign. Veer right onto a mushing trail.

Mi. 2.8   Go right at a "Y" in the trail.

Mi. 3.0   Go right at another "Y." (Both intersections are splits that quickly rejoin the main route.)

Mi. 3.3   Veer left at a "Y." (To the right is Moose Track Trail.) The trail gets wider and a little smoother. Turn right on a singletrack. (The wider route to the left becomes boggy.)

Mi. 3.4   Continue straight where another trail joins from the left. The trail will pass through a grassy area, then widen.

Mi. 3.5   Cross Moose Track Trail. (Left goes to Old Rondy; right to the Science Center.)

Mi. 3.6   Arrive at Science Center Way, where the loop started.

Option

An alternate starting point is where the route crosses the Science Center road at the Coyote Trail. When riding east on the road, turn left at Coyote Trail to begin the ride at Moose Track, mile 2.7 of the route.

North Bivouac

Trails on the north side of Campbell Airstrip Road offer a variety of terrain for mountain bikers. While one is quite well-known, others are not. The Bulldog Trail is known to most area trail users as the Tank Trail. The route offers easier terrain but does require a permit where it enters Fort Richardson Military Reservation. The other routes are the skijoring trails. They offer singletrack opportunities and narrower winter trails that include some ice riding. The frozen ponds lend this part of the park a wilderness feel that is becoming rare in Anchorage's urban landscape.

4-13 Bulldog Trail (Tank Trail)

Difficulty: Easy to moderate depending on distance.

Surface: Midwidth trail becomes very wide. Mostly gravel and hard-packed dirt tread.

Winter: Yes.

Distance: 17.2 miles round trip.

Note: An annual permit is required of all trail users, who must check in before each ride.

Officially known on Fort Richardson as the Bulldog Trail, this route is known by most area trail users by its nickname: the Tank Trail. This gravel and dirt route takes cyclists through a part of Fort Richardson between Arctic Valley Road and the Hillside. With increased security and more training on the post, Army staff are working with the community to allow public access to the trail. Trail users must have a permit to take this route onto post. See Resources to learn how to get a permit. The route is a good choice for early season dirt riding and is open year-round. The area is open to moose hunting in the fall, so avoid the area during the moose season from early September through mid-November.

Before riding, call Fort Rich to confirm that the area is not being used for military exercises or hunting that day. (Be sure to check out after your ride.) The route begins in Far North Bicentennial Park at the North Bivouac trailhead. Mileage starts at the wooden trailhead bollards.

Mi. 0.0 Ride past a red gate, then an information sign. Ride past some smaller trail entrances.

Mi. 0.6 Cross a footbridge over a small creek.

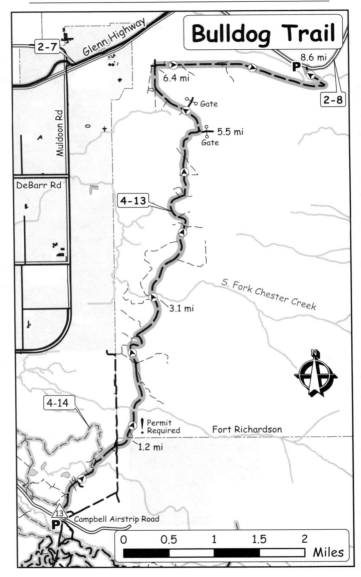

Bulldog Trail

8.6 mi

P

2-7

Glenn Highway

2-8

6.4 mi

Gate

5.5 mi
Gate

Muldoon Rd

DeBarr Rd

4-13

S. Fork Chester Creek

N

3.1 mi

4-14

Fort Richardson

Permit
Required

1.2 mi

13
P Campbell Airstrip Road

0	0.5	1	1.5	2

Miles

Mi. 1.0 At the top of a steep, gravely climb, the trail intersects with the North Gasline Trail, a route that consists of several successive steep climbs and descents.

Mi. 1.2 Cross under a power line as an overgrown trail joins from the right, then pass between two log walls. There is no sign marking the post entry point, but this gateway is on Fort Rich land. Turn around here if you have no permit.

Mi. 1.5 Ride the wooden bridge over the North Fork of Campbell Creek. During the next half mile, notice the warning signs on the right side of the trail alerting you to the possibility of unexploded ordnance. Riders should heed the warnings and stay on the trail.

Mi. 2.3 The main route veers right then uphill. The descent from here will be rocky and often has loose soil.

Mi. 3.1 Cross a wide bridge over the South Fork of Chester Creek and continue.

Mi. 5.3 Arrive at an open area with bogs on both sides of the trail. You'll have a different perspective for viewing the Chugach Mountains, so it's a good place to take in that view.

Mi. 5.5 Go left at a "T." (To the right, a training area beyond the yellow gate is off-limits). The trail widens, with enough room for two vehicles to pass.

Mi. 5.7 Arrive at a cleared area and intersection. Go straight here. (To the right is a second yellow gate, which is also off-limits.)

Mi. 6.4 At this intersection, a sign leading into the area you are leaving reads: "Infantry Squad Battlecourse;

Urban Assault Course; Breach Facility; Shoothouse." Turn right here to ride east. (Straight leads to a dead end at a locked gate.) A buffer of trees on the left separates the trail from the Moose Run Country Club.

Mi. 7.2   Ride past a service entrance for the golf course. In another mile, you'll notice a creek just left of the trail. The trail soon curves left and descends.

Mi. 8.3   Go left at the "T." (Right goes just over a half mile up the trail to a dam on Ship Creek. It also leads to the hiking trail for Snowhawk Cabin.)

Mi. 8.4   Cross a bridge, which has a vehicle gate on the far side, and ride through the parking area.

Mi. 8.6   Go right to stay on the main route and climb a short hill to arrive at the paved portion of Arctic Valley Road. (The sign at this intersection announces the trail-head for the Snowhawk Cabin.) You can turn around here to do the out-and-back ride, or go right to climb up to the Alpenglow ski area (Route 2-8). Left will take you to the Glenn Highway, where you can ride the trail to Anchorage or Eagle River. See Route 2-7 for details.

Skijoring Trails

A trail system you can access from the Tank Trail is the network known as the skijoring trails. Designed for winter use by skiers pulled by one or more dogs, they are maintained by the North American Skijor and Ski Pulk Association (NASSPA) and are considered multi-use. Mountain bikers have discovered this area and use it almost year-round.

The skijor trails appeal to experienced riders who are looking for singletrack and the challenges of rooty, technical trails. Published maps show the winter routes, but not all the winter routes can be traveled during the summer months because they cross bogs and ponds. This guide will cover the routes as they appear during the summer and offer options for winter use.

You can reliably access the trails from two trailheads during the summer: North Bivouac (also referred to as the Tank Trail) and Campbell Airstrip. Winter users shouldn't access these routes from the Airstrip trailhead because it is on a mushing route. The mushing trails are single-use during that season.

4-14 Moose Ridge Loop

Difficulty: Moderate to difficult for the technical nature of the route and lack of signs.

Surface: Mostly singletrack dirt with roots, rocks and possibly logs.

Winter: Yes.

Distance: 2.7-mile loop.

This is one of several singletrack loops you can access from the Bulldog (Tank) Trail. Because there are few signs on the trail, your bike computer will be especially helpful in navigating the route. The mileage for this ride is sometimes expressed in increments of hundredths of a mile. (Differences in computer calibration can cause your mileage to vary.) The route starts at the wooden trailhead bollards.

Mi. 0.0 Ride around the red gate, then turn left away from the Tank Trail. Go right at a "T," then left at a "Y." This is known as the 2.5 Km Loop on skijorer maps. A series of whoop-de-dos will take you quickly down hill.

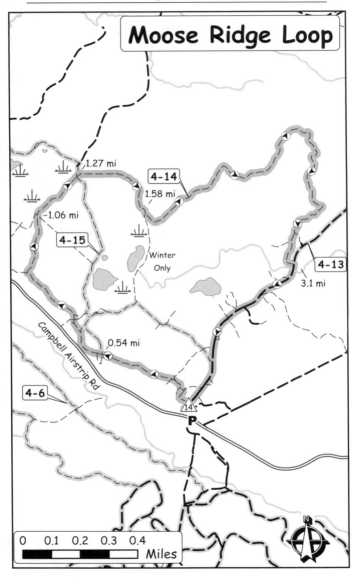

Moose Ridge Loop

1.27 mi

4-14

1.58 mi

-1.06 mi

4-15

Winter
Only

4-13

3.1 mi

Campbell Airstrip Rd

0.54 mi

4-6

14

P

0   0.1   0.2   0.3   0.4

Miles

N

Mi. 0.54 Turn left onto a singletrack at this unmarked intersection. (The main trail stays straight.) The trail climbs along the slope, then falls. Go over a short rise.

Mi. 0.84 Veer right on a descent before riding across two sets of exposed tree roots. Continue descending until you come to an intersection with a trail map.

Mi. 1.06 This intersection is one of the few marked points in the trail system. Continue straight to ride Moose Ridge. Moose Ridge is the longest loop of the system and will take you around several ponds. (To your left, a winter trail crosses a bog; to your right, a trail comes straight downhill toward the intersection.)

Mi. 1.27 Go straight at the next intersection. (To the right, a singletrack winds up the hill; to the left, a rutted trail crosses a wet area and heads back into the trees on the other side of the Beaver Dam mushing trail.)

Mi. 1.58 Stay left at a fork in the trail to avoid a boggy area. (During the winter, NASSPA grooms a route across the pond.) In the spring, some parts of Moose Ridge can be wet or even have water flowing across the trail where some ponds drain to lower areas. This is usually only for short stretches of trail and it's normally dry by mid- to late June.

Continue on the route as the trail climbs and drops and weaves around most boggy areas. Later in the summer parts of the trail can get overgrown with tall grasses and devil's club.

Moose Ridge climbs a short rise and veers left to avoid a bog (right is a winter route). The trail makes a final climb.

Mi. 3.10 Arrive at the Tank Trail and turn right.

Mi. 3.16 Cross a small bridge, then continue toward the trailhead.

Mi. 3.72 Arrive at the trailhead.

Option: 2.1 Km Loop Trail Add-on

You can also ride the 2.1 Km Loop Trail. After leaving Moose Ridge and returning to the Tank Trail, take the second right turn, 0.49 mile from the intersection. (Zero out your computer here.)

Mi. 0.00 Start with a series of whoop-de-dos on this gradual descent.

Mi. 0.21 Stay left at the intersection and approach the edge of the trees.

Mi. 0.35 Turn left on a trail that stays in the trees.

Mi. 0.46 Stay straight on the main singletrack when you see a split to the right. Descend to a wider trail.

Mi. 0.5 Veer left and climb on the wider trail.

Mi. 0.53 Stay on the wide route.

Mi. 0.57 Again, stay on the main trail as another singletrack enters from the left.

Mi. 0.6 Veer left on the main trail where a trail enters from the right and begin climbing.

Mi. 0.73 Stay on the main trail.

Mi. 1.05 Turn left when you arrive at a "Y" intersection.

Mi. 1.12 Turn right onto the Tank Trail.

Mi. 1.2 Arrive at the trailhead bollards.

Winter Option

In winter, instead of turning left at mile 0.35, drop down the steep bank and follow the groomed skijor trail across the frozen pond to connect with mile 1.58 of the Moose Ridge Loop.

4-15   Dogwood Trail**

Difficulty: Moderate to difficult for the technical nature of the route and narrowly spaced trees. There are no signs for finding routes.

Surface: Mostly singletrack with some wider portions. The route has many roots, some mud and possibly logs over the trail.

Winter: In light-snow winters, the route may be rideable. However, at mile 1.78 the route uses a mushing trail that is off-limits. In winter, the roots will be slippery.

Distance: 4.6 miles out and back.

**Dogwood Trail is a name coined by the author.

This singletrack ride starts at the wooden bollards at the North Bivouac trailhead. It includes a portion of the 2.5 Km Loop Trail for just less than half a mile. The route uses a mushing trail for the last half mile, a section you should not ride during the snowy season. Like the previous route, this trail is unmarked. A bike computer is helpful. Again, some mileage is expressed in hundredths of a mile.

Mi. 0.0   Ride around the red gate, then turn left away from the Bulldog (Tank) Trail. Go right at a "T," then left at a "Y." This is the 2.5 Km Loop. A series of whoop-de-dos takes you down hill. Go up a short rise.

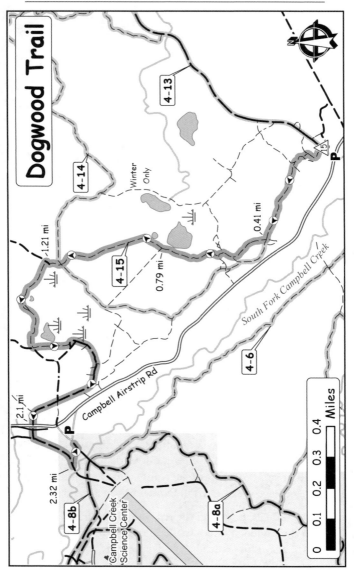

Dogwood Trail

4-13

4-14

Winter Only

1.21 mi

4-15

0.79 mi

0.41 mi

South Fork Campbell Creek

4-6

Campbell Airstrip Rd

2.1 mi

2.32 mi

4-8b

4-8a

Campbell Creek Science Center

Miles

0   0.1   0.2   0.3   0.4

Mi. 0.41 Turn right onto a singletrack that crosses the trail. (It is less noticeable to the left.) This is the Dogwood Trail. Stay on this route, ignoring any offshoot trails.

Mi. 0.54 Connect with a wider main trail and go right, cresting a hill. Look for another singletrack to the left.

Mi. 0.57 Turn left on the singletrack. Stay on the main route, going past a singletrack on the left that leaves the ridge.

Mi. 0.79 Go straight where the Dogwood Trail intersects a wider trail, the 4.5 Km Loop Trail. A pond to the right offers a great view of the Chugach Mountains. Continue on the singletrack.

Mi. 0.82 The trail splits then quickly rejoins, so you can take either option. Both are about the same length. A short descent veers close to the pond. After a short climb, the trail descends from the ridge.

Mi. 1.16 Approach the intersection with Moose Ridge Loop. Cross the trail, then veer right onto a rutted trail informally referred to as Moose Bone Trail.***

***Moose Bone Trail is a name coined by the author and her friends.

Mi. 1.21 Cross the Beaver Dam mushing trail. This section can be damp well into mid-June, so try to stay on the main route to avoid widening the trail. (Yield to sled dogs at this crossing.)

Mi. 1.39 Ride past a large, moss-covered rock on the right side of the trail before climbing a short steep knoll. After descending from the knoll, the trail briefly appears as a doubletrack.

Mi. 1.55 Go left at a split, taking the lower trail as it traverses a side-slope.

Mi. 1.66 Veer left and arrive at a marsh with a view of Wolverine Peak in the background.

Mi. 1.69 Ride alongside the marsh, with a gravel bank to the right. Continue straight, reentering the woods.

Mi. 1.78 Moose Bone merges with the Beaver Dam Trail (entering from the left), although the mushing trail is barely noticeable during the late summer. (Because mushing trails are off-limits during most of the winter, this is a good spot to turn around for an out-and-back route.)

Mi. 1.99 Continue straight at the four-way intersection. (Left will take you directly to Campbell Airstrip Road.)

Mi. 2.11 Ride through a tunnel and head straight across the gravel into another singletrack entrance. This section can be overgrown in mid- to late summer.

Mi. 2.16 Veer left.

Mi. 2.29 Stay right. (Sometimes a split in the trail goes left, but stay right.)

Mi. 2.32 Arrive at a connector trail with two options: Left goes to the Airstrip trailhead parking lot; right goes to the Old Rondy Trail and the Campbell Creek Science Center.

From Campbell Airstrip trailhead

To find this singletrack from the Campbell Airstrip trailhead:

From the bollards of the Campbell Airstrip trailhead, ride to the information sign before the main bridge and take a right onto a narrower, unnamed access trail. At 0.08 mile, look for a hairpin right turn. (If you arrive at a trail along the creek and the mushing bridge, you've gone too far.) The trail entrance is often overgrown even by mid-June and can be easy to miss.

Chapter 5

Chugach State Park

Chugach State Park Rides above the Anchorage Bowl

Chugach State Park is considered to be the backyard for Anchorage's many residents. The 495,000-acre park on the east side of the city has year-round recreation opportunities. A handful of trails are open to mountain biking, and there's even a connector to the trails in Far North Bicentennial Park, allowing cyclists to access the park without driving to a state park trailhead.

During winter months, any areas open to snowmachines are also open to bikes, including the Powerline Trail. Beware of avalanche conditions before venturing onto any steep slopes. In springtime, the state park does not have bike closures during the wet breakup period unless the superintendent decides one is needed to protect the trails. In case of closures, they will be posted at the trailheads.

Routes open to mountain bikes were originally established as road beds, such as the beginning of the Near Point Trail. None of the narrower, singletrack trails in Chugach State Park are open for mountain biking. All biking routes are considered multi-use.

Hikers and climbers often use mountain bikes for quick access to Near Point, Wolverine Peak and Williwaw Lakes, among other destinations. Be sure to stash and lock your bike.

Prospect Heights

5-1   Near Point Trail

Difficulty: Moderate with most climbing on the outbound leg; some large rocks and a water bar.

Surface: Mostly midwidth gravel and dirt.

Winter: Avoid if groomed for skiing only.

Distance: 4.6-mile round trip leads to peak hikes.

Getting to the Trailhead

From the Seward Highway, go east on Dimond Boulevard, which soon becomes Abbott Road. Go past Lake Otis Parkway. Just after the Hillside trailhead, the road curves right and you're now on Hillside Drive. At 4.9 miles, a sign points left for Chugach State Park. Turn left onto Upper O'Malley Road. At a "T," go left on Prospect Drive, then turn left at a stop sign. At the 6.6-mile point, turn right into the parking lot. This is a fee area. The $5 fee can be deposited in the iron ranger payment box. If you have a valid state parks sticker on your vehicle, the fee is waived.

Option

To reach the trailhead from O'Malley Road, go east from the Seward Highway until the road curves left onto Hillside Drive. Take an immediate right onto Upper O'Malley Road and follow the directions above.

This moderate out-and-back route is popular with hikers and trail runners as well as cyclists. The first 2.3 miles

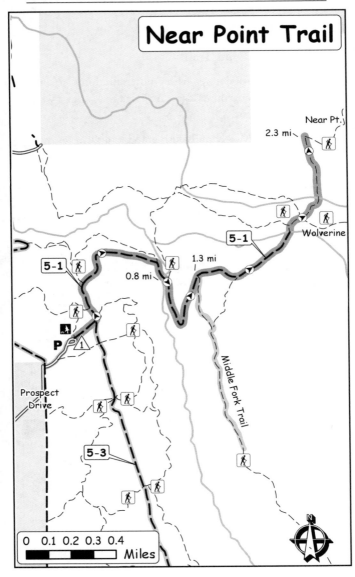

Near Point Trail

2.3 mi
Near Pt.

Wolverine

5-1

1.3 mi

0.8 mi

5-1

P

Prospect
Drive

Middle Fork Trail

5-3

0 0.1 0.2 0.3 0.4

Miles

N

are open to bikes, and signs will tell you where the turn-around point is. It is mostly a climb on the way out, with the return being a fast descent. Be aware of other users on the trail, and respect their right to enjoy the trail without fear of being run over by an out-of-control cyclist! You may prefer to ride this trail during nonpeak times: on weekdays during the day and on weekend evenings.

A side trip out-and-back ride on the Middle Fork trail can be fun, but be aware that the bike turnaround point may not have a sign. Bicycles are not permitted in the back country, but occasionally a cyclist will ride the route after a sign has been destroyed by vandals. This route can be overgrown with cow parsnip by midsummer, so take precautions to avoid the plant, especially on sunny days.

The ride begins at the gate at the trailhead, just east of the outhouse.

Mi. 0.0 Ride the main route, listed on a sign as "Wolverine Bowl Trail." Ride past an information sign on the right.

Mi. 0.1 Turn left at the "T." (Right goes uphill on the Powerline Trail, Route 5-3a). Continue on the main route.

Mi. 0.8 Cross the bridge over the Middle Fork of Campbell Creek and begin climbing on a stretch of trail that is strewn with larger rocks. The trail makes a left switchback.

Mi. 1.3 Go straight. (Turn right to ride the Middle Fork Trail. Bike part way, then stash and lock your bike to hike to Williwaw Lakes.) Cross a small bridge.

Mi. 1.9 Continue straight. (Wolverine Peak Trail branches off to the right. The route is off-limits to bikes, but you can hike to the peak from here.) Cross a small bridge and a log water bar, used to divert water off the trail, before making the final climb.

Mi. 2.3 A trail marker denotes a good turnaround point and resting spot. Farther up the trail is a boardwalk with steps. After the boardwalk, the trail begins to climb and the area is off-limits to bikes.

After a break to rest and look west over Cook Inlet, begin the return trip. Again, watch your speed on the descent.

5-2 Upper Gasline Trail

Difficulty: Difficult due to steepness and loose rocky surface.

Surface: Midwidth dirt and gravel surface with large rocks. Slippery when wet, dusty when dry.

Winter: Not recommended.

Distance: 1.2 miles one way downhill. (For access to the uphill route, see Route 4-7.)

The Upper Gasline is a steep, rocky route that connects Prospect Heights trailhead and the Powerline Trail with the Spencer Loop on the Hillside. Though most of the route is in the municipal park, it appears in this chapter because more riders descend it from the state park. The route is a fast trail with large rocks and a loose surface. Brakes should be in prime condition. Be aware that some riders climb this route because it is the only legal trail connecting the state and municipal parks. Near the end of the route, control your speed as you near the intersection with Spencer Loop.

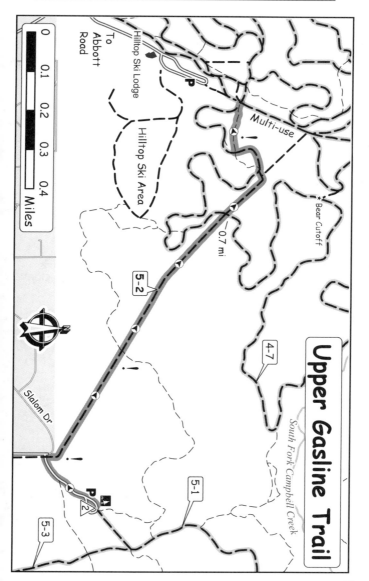

Mi. 0.0 Leave the trailhead parking lot and turn right on Prospect Drive. Prospect ends and you'll ride around a gate, then veer left onto the trail. To ride this descent, pick a line and stay with it. If you slow at the top of each successive hill, you can glance down and pick the route for the next stretch of trail.

Mi. 0.3 Cross the Llama Trail. (Llama goes right to the Near Point Trail or left to the top of Hilltop Ski Area and Spencer Loop.) Continue straight.

Mi. 0.7 Cross Spencer Loop.

Mi. 0.9 Veer left. (Straight is a direct but very steep route to the bottom of the hill.) Enter the lower portion of Spencer Loop, veering right. Complete the last part of Spencer Loop from here, or slow down to prepare to take a steep singletrack. (The mileage listed uses the singletrack.)

Mi. 1.1 Veer right onto an unmarked route that has a short drop-off, then offers a technical descent down a heavily wooded gorge.

Mi. 1.2 Arrive at the end of Spencer Loop, at the Gasline Multi-Use Corridor.

Powerline Trail

The Powerline Pass traverse from Glen Alps to Indian is the most challenging route in the Anchorage area because of the steep descent on the Indian side of the pass. Most riders do this as a more moderate out-and-back ride from Glen Alps, but for more experienced riders who go over the pass, the route offers steep, rocky terrain and rewarding views of Indian Valley and Turnagain Arm.

To traverse the route, wait until midsummer when most of the snowpack has melted on the back side of the pass. The trail will be dryer and the creek crossings not as deep.

Because it is a fairly wide utility route, the trail is easy to follow. If you're going to the pass, watch for an unlabeled turnoff just after a creek crossing in the upper valley at mile 5.1. It isn't always obvious to first-time trail users, so you may miss the crucial intersection that offers the best route to the pass.

The Powerline Trail is also an access route for some area hikes. Biking can cut a few miles off a long hike. (Be sure to lock and stash the bike in the brush.) The area is abundant with wild berries in late summer and early fall, so bring your berry containers for an all-day outing.

Grey Lake is a good destination for out-and-back riders. The area in the upper valley offers alpine lakes and wildflowers, providing a pleasant spot to picnic, hike, view wildlife or relax.

The Powerline Trail is multi-use, so be aware of other users, especially in the first few miles of the trail. Keep alert for bears and moose. Scan the slopes to look for Dall sheep grazing above the valley.

Several trailheads offer access to the Powerline Trail. Listed here are those recommended for cyclists. Each one is in a fee area. The parking fee is $5 per vehicle. There is no charge to park if you have a valid annual state parking pass on you vehicle.

5-3a Prospect Heights to Glen Alps

Difficulty: Moderate to difficult due to strenuous climbing on the way up. Obstacles such as water bars can be hazards for downhill riders.

Surface: Mostly wide gravel with some narrower tread.

Winter: Yes; stay off any areas groomed for skiing only.

Distance: 6 miles round trip.

For mountain bikers who love a good climb, this trailhead offers the longest climb within the state park to Powerline Pass, at 3,500 feet, an elevation gain of 2,385 feet. The first part of the climb is the steepest; don't be discouraged if you have to walk a short stretch.

As you climb, notice a number of narrower singletrack routes on both sides of the trail. According to park officials and the state parks website, these tantalizing trails are off-limits to bikes, so please observe these restrictions.

Getting to the Trailhead

See Route 5-1 for directions.

Begin at the Prospect Heights trailhead and make your way to the far end of the parking lot, near the outhouse.

Mi. 0.0 Ride away from the lot, past an information sign.

Mi. 0.1 Turn right at the "T" and begin a steep climb that intersects the South Fork Rim Trail, a hiking route.

Mi. 0.5 The trail becomes more moderate as it continues climbing and has a few short descents.

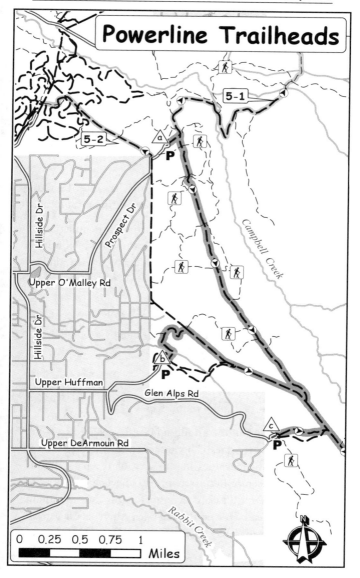

Powerline Trailheads

5-1

5-2

a
P

Hillside Dr

Prospect Dr

Upper O'Malley Rd

Hillside Dr

Campbell Creek

b
P

Upper Huffman

Glen Alps Rd

Upper DeArmoun Rd

c
P

Rabbit Creek

0   0.25   0.5   0.75   1
Miles

N

Mi. 1.5   Intersect again with the South Fork Rim Trail.

Mi. 2.0   After the 2-mile point, approach a large log water bar. It's easy to ride around, but be alert if riding the trail downhill from Glen Alps.

Mi. 2.1   The trail begins to level as Flattop Mountain comes into view.

Mi. 2.5   The trail veers left away from the power lines, then curves right.

Mi. 2.7   Turn left to continue to Glen Alps. (A right turn here goes downhill to the Upper Huffman trailhead.)

Mi. 3.0   At the top of a knoll, arrive at the junction of the Powerline Trail and the Glen Alps trailhead. Continue straight for the pass or turn right to arrive at the trailhead parking lot and the outhouses.

5-3b   Upper Huffman to Glen Alps

Difficulty: Moderate to difficult due to steep grades.

Surface: Mostly wide gravel.

Winter: Yes.

Distance: 4.2 miles round trip.

The Upper Huffman trailhead is often referred to as the "snowmachine trailhead" because it is the only legal access point for snowmachines in this area of the park. It was expanded recently in an attempt to alleviate crowding at Glen Alps. Park officials recommend this as a mountain biking trailhead. However, using Glen Alps cuts off a steep, loose section that may challenge newer riders or children.

Getting to the Trailhead

From the Seward Highway, go east on O'Malley Road, toward the mountains. At mile 3.7, turn right on Hillside Drive. Go one mile, then turn left on Upper Huffman Road, following the signs for the state park. At 5.4 miles, turn left on Sultana Drive. At 5.8 miles, pass a sign for the trailhead. This is a fee area, but the $5 fee is waived if you have a valid state parks sticker on your vehicle. There are a few parking spaces outside the trailhead if the gate is locked.

A few routes leave from the parking lot. The bike route begins at the north end of the lot, opposite the gate.

Mi. 0.0 Ride away from the parking area as the trail drops down, then crosses a wooden bridge before climbing toward a gas pipeline corridor. Stay on the main route.

Mi. 0.6 Arrive at the gasline and turn right to climb.

Mi. 1.0 Continue uphill at a junction with the snow-machine route, which leads back to the Upper Huffman trailhead.

Mi. 1.1 Pass another turnoff on the right as you continue to climb.

Mi. 1.3 The trail levels somewhat before making a final steep, gravely climb to the intersection with the Powerline at 1.8 miles. The route continues to push upward. Stay to the right and be aware of two-way traffic as you go up a steep bank before the trail becomes gradual once again.

Mi. 2.1 Arrive at the intersection with the route coming from the Glen Alps trailhead. Go straight to continue to the pass or turn right to reach the parking lot and outhouses.

5-3c Glen Alps to Indian (Powerline Pass)

Difficulty: Difficult with portions of trail that are steep and off-camber. Large rocks and creek crossings are some obstacles.

Surface: Wide gravel and dirt route.

Winter: Yes, as an out-and-back route, though with avalanche dangers farther up the valley.

Distance: 12.2-mile traverse to Indian or out-and-back to the pass; 9.4-mile round trip to creek crossing.

Glen Alps is the most heavily used trailhead in the Chugach State Park. Because several popular hiking routes begin here, the parking lot can fill on sunny summer days. Don't be tempted to park on the roadway outside the park because it can create a hazard and could block emergency vehicles that are trying to reach the park or homes beyond the trailhead. You may be towed. Instead, use the Upper Huffman trailhead.

Getting to the Trailhead

From the Seward Highway, go east on O'Malley, toward the mountains. At mile 3.7, turn right on Hillside Drive. Go one mile, then turn left on Upper Huffman Road, following the signs for the state park. At 5.4 miles, turn right onto Toilsome Hill Drive. Follow the narrow and sometimes twisting road as it climbs to the trailhead at 7.3 miles. The elevation at Glen Alps is 2,260 feet. This is a fee area, but the $5 fee is waived if you have a valid state parks sticker on your vehicle.

Start at the northeast corner of the parking lot, just left of the steps that lead to Flattop. There are two trails. Bikes are allowed on the left, lower trail.

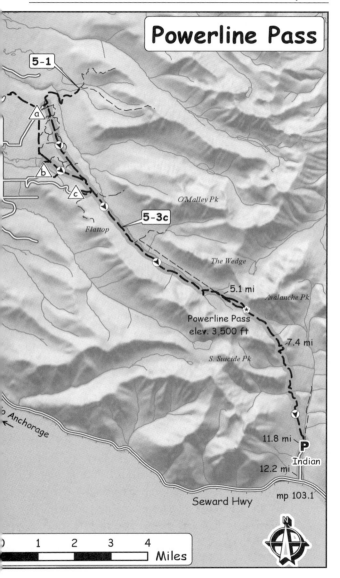

Powerline Pass

5-1

(a)

(b)

(c)

5-3c

O'Malley Pk

Flattop

The Wedge

5.1 mi

Avalanche Pk

Powerline Pass
elev. 3,500 ft

7.4 mi

S. Suicide Pk

to Anchorage

11.8 mi

P
Indian

12.2 mi

Seward Hwy   mp 103.1

N

0   1   2   3   4
Miles

Mi. 0.0 Ride past the gate and veer left to descend to the trail.

Mi. 0.4 Arrive at the Powerline Trail. Turn right to begin riding toward the pass. (Left goes to Upper Huffman and Prospect Heights trailheads.)

Mi. 0.5 Ride past the Middle Fork Loop hiking trail on the left. Continue following the route up the valley.

Mi. 2.3 Pass another hiking trail on the left. (This one leads to Hidden Lake, the Ramp and other hiking destinations. The trail is closed to bikes, but some hikers like to stash their bicycles and hike from here. Lock your bike if you're going to hike.)

Mi. 3.8 Cross a creek and continue climbing as you encounter larger rocks. The trail veers away from the south side of the valley and descends.

Mi. 4.7 Notice the faint hiking trails to the right. These lead to the lakes that feed a creek crossing just ahead. This area makes a good picnic spot for out-and-back riders and invites some exploring on foot. The creek crossing can be over 6 feet wide, but during dry years there may be no water at all. Cross the creek to continue the ride, which climbs immediately from the valley floor.

Mi. 5.1 Turn left on a narrower trail that climbs away from the wider route. (If you continue straight, the wider route continues to climb, then descends before making a steep climb up a rock-covered, very steep slope.) The narrower trail is not marked, but it will briefly pass through some low brush. It then gets steeper and slightly wider as it continues to the pass. There will be loose rocks along the way.

Mi. 6.1   Arrive at Powerline Pass, elevation 3,500 feet. Look back for a view of the valley and Anchorage beyond. Ahead is the Indian Creek Valley. This is the turnaround point for those not wanting to ride or walk the very steep, off-camber switchbacks. Before descending, you may want to lower your bike seat, especially if you want to try to ride the steepest sections of the trail. You may also want to lower your tire pressure to better control the bike on the rocky sections. The descent is steep at first before leveling briefly. The route splits, with a wider route to the right. A narrower route on the left runs parallel.

Mi. 6.6   If you rode the left, narrower option, veer right to rejoin the main route, merging onto a very rocky section of trail. The route follows a slope that even in mid-summer can have snow patches.

Mi. 7.4   Arrive at a level spot with a power pole just left of the trail. From here, see Indian Valley to the left and Turnagain Arm to the right. The steep switchback descent begins here. Even experienced riders have been known to walk portions of the trail for the next mile.

Mi. 8.5   Cross a creek and climb a short distance, then descend more gradually.

Mi. 9.4   Cross another creek and enter an area of tall trees and devil's club.

Mi. 9.6   Enter a more open area where the trail then curves right to continue toward the water.

Mi. 10.6 Continue straight where the Indian Valley hiking trail enters from the left. You may meet more hikers on this portion of trail. The trailhead is now less than a mile away.

Mi. 11.3 Cross a pair of creeks.

Mi. 11.5 Pedal around the trailhead gate and continue straight.

Mi. 11.8 Turn right onto Ocean View Road.

Mi. 12.2 Arrive at the Seward Highway, mile 103.1 (23.9 miles from downtown Anchorage). Turnagain House is on the left. This is a good place to meet people if you have a ride back to Anchorage. To pedal back to Anchorage, turn right onto the highway. The wide shoulder gives enough room for cyclists to ride single file on the pavement. From here, you'll ride almost 15 miles to the Rabbit Creek Road off-ramp, milepost 117.8.

Option

To return to Glen Alps, turn right onto Potter Valley Road, milepost 115.4, just after the Chugach State Park Headquarters at the Potter Section House. Turn left almost immediately onto the Old Seward Highway. Turn right onto Rabbit Creek Road and climb. After passing the intersection with DeArmoun Road, continue on Hillside Drive. Turn right on Upper Huffman Road, following the signs back to the trailhead.

Out and Back Riders

The creek crossing at Grey Lake makes a good turn-around point. It's also a great place for a picnic lunch or a hike in the valley. (Look for small hiking trails that leave the Powerline Trail to the right on either side of the crossing.) Another option is to complete the climb to the top of the pass before turning around and heading back to the trailhead. It's a beautiful view as you descend, so be sure to stop and take it all in.

Chapter 6

South to Girdwood

Indian to Bird Point to Girdwood

The popular "Bird to Gird" Trail was extended west to Indian in 2004. The original route between Bird Point and Girdwood follows the former roadbed of the Seward Highway and is popular for locals and visitors. Rising away from the highway, it offers several viewpoints and informational signs, plus picnic areas and outhouses.

In early spring, some portions of the route may be covered by avalanche debris. If there is any chance of a late winter snowslide, park officials will not open this trail. Riders should heed any closures for their safety.

Bike rentals are available in Girdwood, and cyclists can ride from the shop to the eastern trailhead. See Resources for more information.

The newer, western portion of trail connects an existing trail at Indian with Bird Point. Although the trail didn't officially open until 2005, bikers began riding part of this route in late 2004. Until construction on the Bird Creek parking area is complete, start the route just east of Bird Creek, about 1.7 miles into this description. When the trail opens, riders can begin at the Indian Creek parking lot on the south side of the highway at milepost 103, just past the Turnagain House restaurant. This is sure to be a popular starting point for Anchorage residents wanting a shorter drive and a longer bike ride.

The drive along Turnagain Arm can be one of the most scenic trips in the Anchorage area, and the Seward Highway is recognized by the National Scenic Byways Program. The highway was completed in 1951 and is the only driving route connecting the Kenai Peninsula with Anchorage, the state's largest city.

It is normally busy on summer weekends as people leave town for their favorite recreation spots on the Peninsula. It is especially busy when the salmon are running. People often slow down or pull to the side of the highway to view beluga whales in the Arm or Dall sheep on the cliffs that border the road to the north. For wildlife viewing, use one of the highway turnouts. Remember to keep your headlights on at all times while driving the Seward Highway.

Even without the wildlife viewing, the Seward Highway is scenic for the tree-covered mountains. Spring here arrives a few weeks earlier than in the Anchorage Bowl. The trees on the south-facing slopes bud early in the spring, when much of Anchorage still has snow. In fall, the leaves turn to yellow and red after most trees in the Anchorage Bowl have shed their leaves, offering a last breath of fall before the long winter.

Turnagain Arm experiences some of the most extreme tides in North America, and it's common for people to make an outing of watching the wall of water, known as a bore tide, rush into the narrow Arm. Consult tide tables to learn when the tides will be most dramatic. A good viewing spot is at Bird Point about 45 minutes after low tide in Anchorage. Don't be tempted to walk toward the waterline when the tide is out, because the silty soil can act like quicksand and trap a person. The suction is so strong that you may not be able to extract yourself before the tide rushes in.

High winds can sweep through this area, which is bounded by the Chugach Mountains to the north and the Kenai Mountains across the water to the south. Road bikers are always aware of the strong, shifting winds, and most conversations about a ride along this scenic route begin with a comment on whether the cyclist had headwinds, tailwinds or both.

Some parts of the bike path from Indian to Girdwood offer shelter from the wind, but several areas are exposed, so pack your windbreaker. You may even want to bring wind pants.

6-1a Indian to Bird Point

Difficulty: Easy to moderate depending on the wind.

Surface: Paved.

Winter: No. This trail goes past chutes that avalanche every year.

Distance: 14.2 miles round trip (26.2 miles round trip when combined with Route 6-1b).

Getting to the Trailhead

From Anchorage, drive south on the Seward Highway. From the Rabbit Creek overpass, drive another 15 miles. Just after the Turnagain House, cross a short bridge over Indian Creek and turn right into the parking lot at milepost 103 (about 15.1 miles from the overpass). There's limited parking, so it's best to carpool from Anchorage. Mileage for this route begins at the trailhead bollards, where the trail leaves the parking lot driveway.

Mi. 0.0   Ride east. The trail soon veers away from the highway.

Mi. 1.1   Arrive at the Bird Creek fishing area, then descend and cross a bridge.

Mi. 1.6   Arrive at the Bird Creek Campground day-use parking area. There is very limited parking here, but

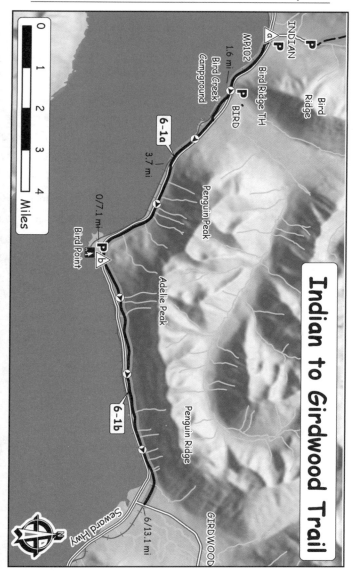

Indian to Girdwood Trail

179

more is available across the highway. Ride past the camp-ground, in a wooded area.

Mi. 2.0 Ride past an intersection. This left turn leads to the outbound driveway for the campground and inter-sects the Seward Highway at Sawmill Road. The Essential 1 gas station is across the highway to the left; the Bird Ridge Cafe & Bakery is to the right.

Mi. 2.4 Veer right to cross a bridge. (To the left, a tunnel goes under the highway.)

Mi. 3.0 Veer close to a highway pullout before descending closer to the water and the railroad tracks.

Mi. 3.7 Pass a gravel maintenance road, then ride through a tunnel. On the far side of the tunnel, the path will become fairly straight and level for a time. The grade is higher than the road and frequently is windy.

Mi. 5.4 Cross an access road and begin a gradual climb to a viewpoint. From here, the route meanders, then begins a descent.

Mi. 6.6 Cross another access road. Across the highway is the vehicle entrance to the Bird Point parking lot. Cross one more access driveway.

Mi. 7.1 Arrive at the intersection with the Bird Point access route. Go straight to continue to Girdwood. Turn right to reach the Bird Point parking lot, or return the way you came.

6-1b   Bird Point to Girdwood (Bird to Gird)

Difficulty: Easy to moderate with one long hill each way; can be windy.

Surface: Paved.

Winter: No. Route goes through several dangerous avalanche slide areas.

Distance: 12 miles round trip. (26.2 miles round trip when combined with Route 6-1a.)

This route has a number of points of interest. Signs along the trail refer to the area's history and some sights you will see from the trail. The mileage listed is independent of the previous section.

To get to the trailhead, continue six miles past the Indian trailhead identified in 6-1a. Turn right, toward the water, into the Bird Point parking lot at milepost 96.5. The parking fee is $5, but there is no additional fee for those with a valid state parks annual parking sticker.

The paved trail begins at the northeast corner of the parking area, just left of an information sign. Ride under the highway and up a hill to the intersection with the main trail. The mileage begins at the wooden signpost.

Mi. 0.0   Go right to climb the trail. Notice several viewpoints along the way.

Mi. 0.5   A retired avalanche gun is displayed to the right.

Mi. 0.9   The rest area on the right features outhouses and a picnic area.

Mi. 1.4   Enter an avalanche slide zone. (Note the

absence of many mature trees upslope.) The display on the left describes different kinds of snowslides.

Mi. 2.0 Just past the two-mile point is the top of the climb and the beginning of a gradual descent.

Mi. 3.8 Arrive at the second picnic and rest area. Continue descending.

Mi. 4.0 After the bottom of the hill, notice the Alaska Railroad tracks to your right, between the trail and the highway. The rail line connects Seward and Whittier to Anchorage. For your safety, don't trespass on the tracks, which are active with freight and passenger trains.

Mi. 4.5 A display on the left describes the avalanche dangers faced during the building of the railroad, between 1904 and 1922, before the highway existed.

Mi. 5.0 After the five-mile point, the trail shoulder becomes steep and narrow as you enter the Tidewater Slough, a tidal marsh that was created when the 1964 earthquake caused the land here to sink 8 feet and soaked the forest, which stands today as dead spruce in a sea of marsh plants. This area is good for birdwatching.

Mi. 5.4 Cross a bridge over a channel. A display on the far side of the bridge tells more about the slough.

Mi. 5.5 Leave state park land and enter municipal land.

Mi. 5.7 At a stop sign, cross the road and veer left, then right to continue on the trail.

Mi. 6.0 Meet the Alyeska Highway. To the right is the Seward Highway. There's an ice cream shop and a couple of restaurants at the intersection. Turn left to ride to the heart of Girdwood and more restaurants. The U.S. Forest Service ranger station is just up the road on the left. The bike rental shop is also to the left, at mile 1.5 of the Alyeska Highway, or 1.3 miles from this junction.

Girdwood Area

Much of the biking available in the Girdwood area is on pavement. Few continuous dirt routes exist, however a new option, downhilling at Alyeska, is available for riders seeking more thrills.

6-2 Alyeska Downhill

Difficulty: Difficult with very steep off-camber routes and loose soil.

Surface: Dirt and gravel with obstacles including jumps.

Winter: No.

Distance: Less than 1 mile each route.

In the summer of 2004, Downhill Division at Alyeska Resort offered the first lift-served downhill mountain biking in the Anchorage area and Alaska. Beginning with just two runs, the operators hope to add more trails. Current courses almost require riders use a downhill-specific bike, one with lots of travel, wider tires and a very low seat. Rentals are available at Downhill Division. Bike shops in Anchorage sell downhill-specific bikes if you decide this kind of riding is for you.

Getting to the Trailhead

Drive south from Anchorage on the Seward Highway. From the Rabbit Creek overpass in South Anchorage drive

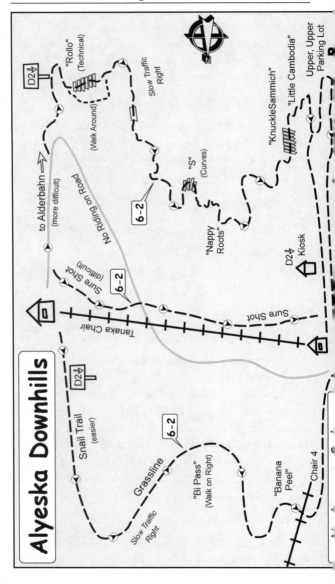

Alyeska Downhills

to Alderbahn ⇒ (more difficult)

"Rollo" (Technical)

(Walk Around)

Slow Traffic Right

"S" (Curves)

"KnuckleSammich"

"Little Cambodia"

Upper, Upper Parking Lot

"Nappy Roots"

Kiosk

No Riding on Road

Sure Shot (difficult)

Tanaka Chair

Sure Shot

Snail Trail (easier)

Grassline

"Bi Pass" (Walk on Right)

Slow Traffic Right

"Banana Peel"

Chair 4

28 miles to the intersection with the Alyeska Highway, milepost 90. Turn left and drive toward the mountains. After three miles, go right at a "T." (Left goes to the Alyeska Prince Hotel.) Park in the gravel lot and walk to the kiosk, just right of the Tanaka chair lift. This is where riders purchase lift tickets and get outfitted with their rental bikes and protective gear.

Ride the chair lift up the mountain, where you can see parts of the trails. At the top of the lift, an access route goes left to the 3,100-foot-long, easier Snail Trail. To the right is the more challenging Alderbahn, which is 2,500 feet long and has numerous obstacles. A third route, Sure Shot, parallels the lift. Routes and trail surfaces may change as this biking area evolves, and the staff will advise riders on where to start and provide a description of what to expect.

None of the routes available in 2004 would be rated easy. They are all for experienced riders who are looking for a downhill experience. The season is expected to run weekends from June 1 through the end of August, but call ahead to be sure. See Resources for detailed information.

Chapter 7

Northeast of the Anchorage Bowl

Northeast of the Anchorage Bowl you'll find some excellent rides that are quickly accessible for those who live in communities from Eagle River to Eklutna. They are easy to get to from the Glenn Highway and worth checking out. The trails are diverse, from ski loop trails that offer a variety of difficulties of terrain to singletrack trails to wide, gravel trails. All the trails described here are multi-use in the summer and worth exploring.

Beach Lake Nordic Ski Trails (Chugiak Ski Trails)

The ski trails on this mostly well-marked trail system provide challenging transitions between descending and gearing down for the climbs as they twist through a wooded park near Chugiak High School. Expect trails to open to bicycles by June 1. In dry conditions, watch out for sand pits on the trail. Some hills can have loose rocks. Conditions vary throughout the season and from one year to the next.

Getting to the Trailhead

Go north on the Glenn Highway. From the Muldoon Road overpass drive north 12.5 miles. Just after the sign for Chugiak, take the South Birchwood exit, milepost 17.2, and turn left at the stop sign. Birchwood Loop Road goes under the highway. Turn right into the first driveway for the school parking lot, then turn left. Continue to the far end of the lot, near the athletic fields. Be sure to observe any parking restrictions during the school year.

Park on the west side of the school. Look north toward the playing fields. The trailhead is just west of the fields, past a guardrail and concrete barricades. An information sign with a map is on your left. A new trailhead and chalet were built by the local ski club less than half a mile beyond the high school on Birchwood Loop. The trail from the chalet to the Beach Lake system was completed in the fall of 2004, and it accesses the system at mile 1.1 of the Green Trail.

The routes are color coded to correspond with the map at the trailhead. You can download the color map from the Nordic Skiing Association of Anchorage (NSAA) website for an easier read (see Resources).

Maps are coded red, green or blue. This route follows the red trail, also listed as the 10 Km Loop. Follow trails that list either of these on the signs. Some routes are marked with more than one color. The 10 Km Loop is the most challenging route, so you may choose other routes based on your energy level. Besides being color coded, shapes are incorporated into the design of the signs. Red is a diamond, blue a square and green a circle.

7-1a   Red Trail

Difficulty: Moderate. The route has steep hills with some loose sand and rocks.

Surface: Wide grass and dirt.

Winter: No.

Distance: 6.4-mile loop.

Mi. 0.0   Begin at the concrete trailhead barriers, riding past the trail sign, through the outbound tunnel and around a red gate.

Mi. 0.2   At a three-way split, take the middle route and begin climbing. (Left is the inbound route; right is the Low Road of the Green Trail.) Continue straight, passing a pair of connector routes.

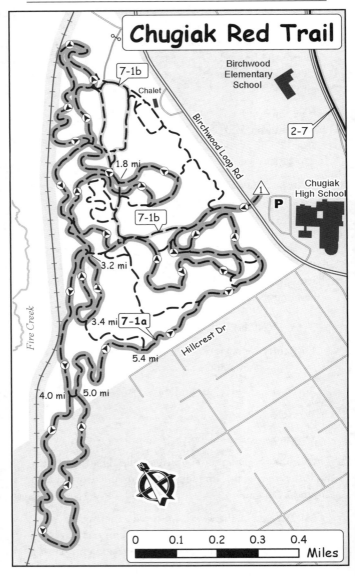

Chugiak Red Trail

Birchwood Elementary School

7-1b

Chalet

2-7

Birchwood Loop Rd

1.8 mi

1

Chugiak High School

P

7-1b

3.2 mi

Fire Creek

3.4 mi 7-1a

Hillcrest Dr

5.4 mi

4.0 mi 5.0 mi

0	0.1	0.2	0.3	0.4

Miles

Mi. 0.5   Go right at a fork to enter the Luge.

Mi. 0.9   After descending, enter an open area and ride to the left of a sign with a trail map, then continue straight.

Mi. 1.0   Just after the 1-mile mark, turn right and descend on the Bridge Loop.

Mi. 1.1   Continue straight, following the red diamonds. (Left returns to parking.)

Mi. 1.3   Stay right to ride to the Corral Loop. (Left is Bridge Loop shortcut.) At a four-way intersection, go straight to begin the Corral Loop. You'll soon see a sign for the 10 Km route.

Mi. 1.5   Go left to stay on Corral.

Mi. 1.8   At the end of the Corral Loop, an arrow points right for the green route. Turn right, then take an immediate left onto the red route. Continue straight at a four-way intersection.

Mi. 2.0   Take the farthest right option to enter the Junkyard. The sandy areas on this part of the trail system make bike handling a little more challenging, especially in dry conditions.

Mi. 2.2   Veer left and see a sign for the 10 Km route.

Mi. 2.7   The Alaska Railroad tracks are visible to the right before you climb the next hill.

Mi. 2.8   Junkyard ends. Stay right to ride more of the Bridge Loop.

Mi. 3.1   Cross a plank bridge, then climb, veering right.

Mi. 3.2   Arrive at a crossroad and go straight. This

loop is known as the Appendix. (To bypass the Appendix, make a sharp right turn.)

Mi. 3.4   Veer right to stay on the Red route and descend a sometimes loose, rocky leg of the trail. (Straight is Coach's Cutoff, which cuts off two miles of the route.)

Mi. 3.6   Go left. (You're at the end of Appendix.)

Mi. 4.0   Continue straight to ride the Hill Loop with its steep terrain and areas of large, loose rocks.

Mi. 5.0   Turn right at the end of Hill Loop. Keep right at a junction to ride the slightly wider Blue route, and climb Agony Hill.

Mi. 5.4   Go straight. (To the left is the end of Coach's Cutoff.)

Mi. 5.6   Stay right at this and the next intersection.

Mi. 5.8   Keep left at the intersection, then straight at the next one.

Mi. 5.9   Pass a sign for YoYos and begin a climb. YoYos includes some fun ups and downs, with wide sweeping turns.

Mi. 6.1   Veer right as the trail curves right and descends. Continue straight as you arrive at Main Street.

Mi. 6.3   Arrive at the trail gate. Ride around the gate and through the inbound tunnel to finish the ride.

Mi. 6.4   End at the concrete barriers.

7-1b Green Trail

Difficulty: Easy with just a few small hills.

Surface: Wide, mostly grassy surface with some loose gravel.

Winter: No.

Distance: 2.1-mile loop.

The Green Trail is an easier route, making it a good alternative for new riders and kids who have geared bikes. Some trails built in the summer and fall of 2004 lead to the new ski chalet on Birchwood Loop. This route also begins at the concrete barriers near the Chugiak High athletic fields.

Mi. 0.0 Ride past the trail information sign, through the outbound tunnel and around the trailhead gate.

Mi. 0.2 Veer right at a three-way split. This is known as the Low Road.

Mi. 0.3 Keep right as you join the Red and Blue routes in the area known as Crossroads. Ride to the right of the trail map sign, then veer right to follow the Green route. Make a moderate, yet somewhat rocky descent.

Mi. 0.4 Stay straight to pass Mama's Loop. Ride past a trail that enters from the right, then arrive at a four-way intersection

Mi. 0.5 Turn right onto the Corral Loop. (Straight would go directly to the North Pasture.) Corral is also part of the Red loop.

Mi. 0.9 At the end of Corral, turn right to follow the Green route, then go straight. Take the right fork where

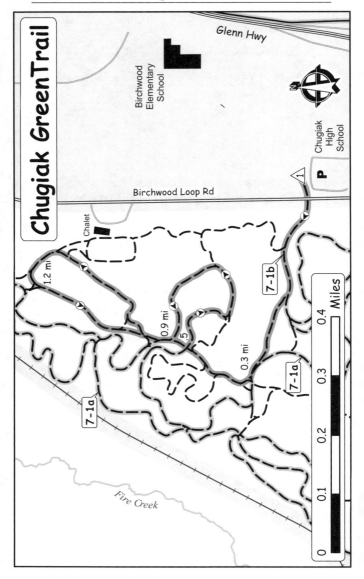

Chugiak Green Trail

194

the trail splits. Much of the trail has been in a stand of mostly birches, but now notice more spruce. The trail surface may be a little wet and bumpier than other sections of the trail.

Mi. 1.1   Continue straight as a new trail breaks away to the right. (The new trail was completed in the late fall of 2004 and leads to the new ski chalet and parking area on Birchwood Loop Road.)

Mi. 1.2   Keep to the far left to finish the North Pasture. The trail can be confusing here because the Junkyard and North Pasture trails meet, plus a third trail leading out of the park and onto an access road joins here. This route isn't shown on the trail maps posted throughout the trail system.

Mi. 1.5   Rejoin the outbound route and continue straight, keeping right for the Green route. Continue past the next intersection, Corral Loop.

Mi. 1.6   Ride straight through a four-way intersection. (The beginning of Corral is on the left; Bridge Loop is to the right.) Stay left at a split, cross a creek and continue straight.

Mi. 1.7   Arrive at the Crossroads intersection and stay to the far left to return on the Low Road, arriving once again at Main Street, where you'll stay left.

Mi. 2.0   Return to the gate. Ride through the tunnel and past the information sign.

Mi. 2.1   End at the concrete barriers.

Chugach State Park Trails

Northeast of the Anchorage Bowl, cyclists will find two routes within the Chugach State Park that are open to riding. Both rides are unique and provide inviting escapes from the more urban trails. Eklutna Lakeside Trail is well used and offers some of the prettiest scenery for the least amount of effort. Peters Creek Trail, while shorter, has more challenging climbs. It sees less use so is more likely to be overgrown during the middle of summer.

7-2   Peters Creek Trail

Difficulty: Moderate, with a long climb and some steep areas.

Surface: Wide gravel route becomes narrower with some singletrack dirt. Creek crossing.

Winter: Yes, on snowmachine routes. Beware of avalanche dangers.

Distance: 10.4-mile round trip.

This out-and-back ride in Chugach State Park offers a taste of singletrack that is convenient to riders in the Eagle River area. The route is well established and is especially scenic during the early fall when the birches turn yellow and the first snow has fallen on the peaks across the creek valley. This part of the park is also open to hunting in the fall, so don't be surprised to meet hunters along the way.

Getting to the Trailhead

From Anchorage, drive north on the Glenn Highway. From the Muldoon Road overpass, drive 17 miles to the South Peters Creek exit, milepost 21.5. Turn right to drive east up Ski Road. Follow Ski Road to Whaley Avenue and

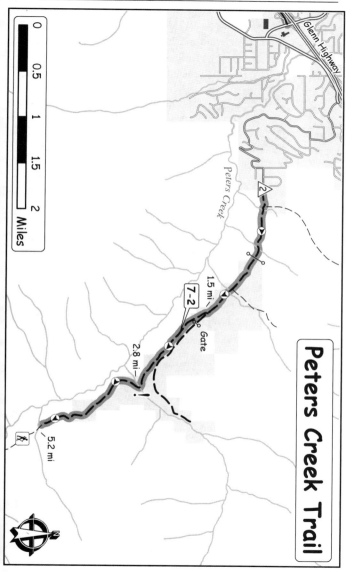

Peters Creek Trail

turn right. Whaley makes a 90-degree left turn to become Chugach Park Drive. Follow Chugach Park Drive up the mountain. Turn left on Kullberg Drive, then take an immediate right onto Sullins Drive, which climbs up a switchback. Turn right on Malcolm Drive. The trailhead is just up the hill where Malcolm intersects with Sierra Mesa Circle.

Parking is limited, so it's best to carpool and park as far onto the shoulder as possible. The trailhead is at the corner and marked with an information sign.

Mi. 0.0 Begin where the dirt trail leaves the pavement. Ride the doubletrack as it becomes somewhat steep.

Mi. 0.7 Ride around a gate and continue climbing the dirt and gravel route.

Mi. 1.3 Ride past the entrance to a hiking route for Bear Mountain on the left. Though off-limits to bicycles, this makes a good day hike. After a descent, approach a gate spanning the trail.

Mi. 1.5 Just before the gate, turn right to drop down a short steep hill onto the slightly narrower trail. The tread on this descent can be rocky with a loose surface, so use care. Follow the route as the tread becomes more of a singletrack in a grassy trail corridor.

Mi. 2.6 An arrow in the woods on the left points the way.

Mi. 2.8 Arrive at the Fourmile Creek crossing. Water can be ice cold even during the summer. It's fairly shallow, so skilled riders should be able to ride across the creek, which is about 15 feet wide at this spot. Farther upstream, trail users have placed logs across a narrower span of the creek for those who want to keep their feet dry. Be aware of ice on the logs during fall rides.

After crossing the creek, the trail climbs a bank, then veers right. The route continues its gradual climb up the valley, past a meadow and back into the woods.

Mi. 5.2 The biking route ends when you arrive at a wooden post with a sign that shows no biking after this point. Hikers can stash and lock their bikes to continue another 11 plus miles up the valley on foot for a long day-hike. Be sure to bring an area map.

The return trip will be faster since the route climbed most of the way. Keep your bike under control and watch for other trail users.

7-3   Eklutna Lakeside Trail

Difficulty: Easy to moderate depending on distance traveled. Some steep sections, but mostly a gradual climb up the valley.

Surface: Mostly wide gravel with options for narrower side trails. Some steep sections.

Winter: Yes. Beware of avalanche dangers.

Distance: 25.4-mile round trip.

The Lakeside Trail at Eklutna is popular with bikers, hikers, equestrians and off-road vehicle users. In the winter, it's open to snowmachiners and other users, but it does experience avalanches. The route rewards riders with some of the best scenery for the effort. The wide gravel and dirt trail skirts the north side of the lake. The route is exposed to early season sunshine, drying the surface. This makes Eklutna one of the first places for cyclists to enjoy off-road riding each spring.

For the first 7.5 miles, there are often two trail options: one for motorized users and one for nonmotorized users, including bicycles. The lower, nonmotorized, trail offers a better view of the lake and a variety of surfaces. Much of it is hard packed, although parts can be muddy, rooty or even rocky with loose sand. But it is less steep, so it's an easier ride than the upper trail.

The trail is open to ATVs Sunday through Wednesday. It is open to all non-motorized users seven days a week. If you prefer riding when motorized vehicles aren't present, plan your rides for Thursday through Saturday. Otherwise, stay alert when the trails are shared by all users, including motorized vehicles.

Some amenities at the trailhead include a campground, outhouses, bike and kayak rentals and drinking water. There are two public-use cabins along the trail available for rental, and two campgrounds near the head of the lake. The area offers not just biking and kayaking, but also several day hikes, so there are a number of reasons to spend the night at a rustic cabin or campground.

Getting to the Trailhead

Drive north on the Glenn Highway. About 20 miles past the Muldoon overpass, take the Thunderbird Falls exit, milepost 25.2. Go north, past the parking lot for the falls. At 21.3 miles, turn right onto Eklutna Lake Road. In two miles, the road narrows and no longer has a shoulder. This newly paved stretch of road sits atop a high roadbed. It is curvy in places as it climbs to the lake. If you're riding your bike to the trail, dress brightly and be aware of the possible hazards, including wide motor homes or vehicles with trailers.

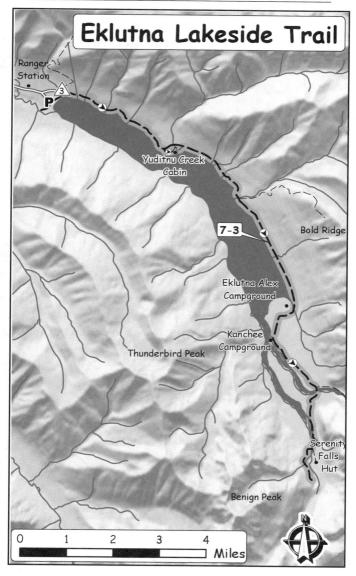

Eklutna Lakeside Trail

Ranger Station

P

Yuditnu Creek Cabin

Bold Ridge

7-3

Eklutna Alex Campground

Kanchee Campground

Thunderbird Peak

Serenity Falls Hut

Benign Peak

| 0 | 1 | 2 | 3 | 4 | Miles |

N

Just before milepost 8 are Cheely's General Store and Rochelle's Ice Cream Shop. Cabin rentals and showers are available. In another mile, arrive at the fee station. If no one is at the station, continue past the campground and turn right into the day-use parking area. Pay your $5 parking fee at the iron ranger fee box. No additional fee is needed for those with a valid annual state parks parking pass.

When returning to Anchorage, turn right at the end of Eklutna Lake Road and follow the signs to the Glenn Highway on-ramp. You'll enter the highway at milepost 26.3.

This description will follow the nonmotorized routes where ever they exist and begins at the east side of the day-use parking area.

Mi. 0.0 From a sign for the Twin Peaks and Lakeside trails, ride past a long-handled water pump and cross a bridge over Twin Peaks Creek. At the intersection, turn right to take the Lakeside Trail. (Straight will take you to Lifetime Adventures, a company that rents bikes and kayaks at the lake. They also have drinks, snacks and trail maps.) The trail curves left and passes some benches facing the water.

Mi. 0.3 Go right onto a narrower trail. This is the first of the nonmotorized routes along the trail. Soon it will rejoin the main trail.

Mi. 0.9 Pass milepost 1. The mileage on the posts may differ slightly from your computer reading because of the different routes. The side trails don't have their own mileposts, so you'll miss many of them in the early part of the ride.

Mi. 1.2   Veer right for the next side trail. This route offers some more challenging terrain in a very short rooty, twisty section. It may present a challenge to newer riders, children or those hauling camping gear. Continue riding, taking the side trails whenever possible.

Mi. 2.6   This right turn ultimately leads to first cabin. First, it climbs next to a creek and crosses a bridge before taking another right turn and descending.

Mi. 3.2   As the tail curves left, the cabin is on the right.

Mi. 5.0   Cross Bold Creek on a wooden bridge. Upstream, notice some large trees that were uprooted in the late 1990s during fall storms. The storms washed out some bridges, which have since been replaced. Immediately after the bridge, on the left is the beginning of the Bold Ridge hiking trail. Ride two more side trails before reentering the main route.

Mi. 7.6   Go right on the main route and climb, then take a descent with wide curves. The trail veers left and enters an avalanche zone from a slide that occurred in early 2000. An aged, scarred cottonwood tree stands on the right side of the trail. Looking upslope, witness the new growth filling in the hillside and a couple of stands of trees that were spared during the avalanche. Ride past more evidence of the powerful slide as you continue along the trail and cross Eight Mile Creek.

Mi. 8.3   Veer left. (Right leads to the Bold Airstrip.) You're now at the head of the lake. The route can be sandy and rocky in dry years, but it may have standing water in puddles. After a rain, expect the rocks to be slippery.

Mi. 8.7 Eklutna Alex Campground is to the right in this generally flat area.

Mi. 10.3 Arrive at the East Fork Trail, a hiking route that follows the river upstream. Tulchina Falls is just two miles up the trail. Veer right and cross a bridge over the East Fork of Eklutna River. The river is gray with glacial silt and has a strong current as it flows to the lake.

On the far side of the river, the trail can be rocky, with a very loose surface. It also narrows.

Mi. 10.9 Arrive at the Kanchee (porcupine) Campground. Continue as the trail remains bumpy, with large rocks. The valley narrows.

Mi. 11.3 Riding near the cliffs on the left, notice boulders from landslides resting on both sides of the trail. Eklutna Glacier comes into view ahead.

Mi. 11.8 Arrive at Serenity Falls cabin (straight). Veer right to continue, crossing the West Fork of Eklutna River.

Mi. 12.1 A view of Serenity Falls is on the right. Up ahead on the trail, water at a creek crossing is fed by the falls.

Mi. 12.7 Arrive at the end of the route that allows motorized use. Riders can continue along a singletrack past a sign, but they soon will have to leave their bikes behind and approach carefully to get a closer look at the glacier. The rock face will be slippery for those wearing bike shoes, so bring other shoes to hike past a rocky section.

The return trip is much faster because the route now descends slightly. Take time to enjoy the views on the way back to the trailhead.

Chapter 8

Winter Bicycling

Roots

While winter biking seems like a new phenomenon, it has been a part of Alaska since the late 1800s. Accounts of gold rush stampeders riding and sometimes carrying their bikes down the frozen Yukon River and other winter routes inspire cyclists today. Bike-riding stampeders, while not as prevalent as mushers with dogsleds, pointed out that when they were done for the day, they didn't have to cook for their dog team. They did, however, worry that the grease in their hubs would freeze in the subzero temperatures and that they would be injured in a spill on the ice.

Today, elite winter cyclists race in events that follow the frozen Iditarod Trail, the route of the famous sled dog race each March between Anchorage and Nome. The unusual events, such as the Iditarod Trail Invitational and the Susitna 100, pit cyclists, skiers, snowshoers and runners against one another in a human-powered challenge of mental and physical endurance. Yet Mother Nature determines who has the best chance of winning.

With just a few modifications and some key equipment, recreational cyclists can enjoy the multi-use trails around Anchorage virtually all winter. Conditions can range from ice to light snow to snow that is a foot or more deep. Many Anchorage mountain bikers are also enthusiastic skiers or snowboarders, but in low-snow years or when the trails are packed, conditions can be perfect for biking. Many dedicated skiers have turned to biking to get through a snowless, dark winter.

It's essential that you take the proper precautions, use appropriate gear and remain safety conscious about the effects of the extreme cold. Even when you're traveling only a few miles from home, the perils of the cold winter can pose a danger. You should always be prepared to handle the low temperatures and mechanical problems.

Bicycle

Choose a frame that fits you well and will accommodate your choice of wheels. Some people will use the same bike as they do in the summer, but be aware that if you're doing endurance racing or have any concerns about equipment not working as well in the winter, you may need more specialized equipment.

Suspension

Many older forks, especially those that rely on elastomer (rubberlike) springs, will stiffen in the cold. You may be able to replace the elastomers with metal springs or forgo the front suspension entirely. Local shops sell rigid forks for this reason.

Some newer bike models with rear suspension use air-sprung shocks. In extreme temperatures, seals may fail, causing the shock to leak. Check your rear shock before each ride or consider using a rigid frame if you're consistently out in the cold or have problems with a leaking shock. See the Resources for bike shops that can offer advice.

Tires

For ice riding, most people rely on studded tires, which have been available commercially for several years. Tires can have up to 300 carbide-tipped studs each, which will improve your traction and confidence on the ice. The studded tires work especially well for commuting, when you know you'll be on the roadway. Icy spells vary from year to year, so pay close attention to the trail conditions.

Rims

Many riders use their summer rims year-round. Standard rims are 20 to 25 mm wide. If you're riding in snow, lower the tire pressure or use wider rims. A popular Alaska rim is the SnowCat. At 44 mm wide, it gives the tire a wider footprint, giving the rider more float. This allows the rider to pedal in softer conditions and on fresh snow without sinking in very deep. But if the snow is more than 5 or 6 inches deep, get out your skis! This is Alaska, after all, and you can ride again after the snow gets packed down.

Tires for Wider Rims

Local shops will stock tires with up to a 2.5-inch tread width to go with your rims. It's critical that you make sure the rim and tire combination will fit on your bike frame. If there is any rubbing and you ride that way for too long, you will ruin your frame as the rubber wears through the metal. Shops may recommend you bring your bike in so they can test the combination in your frame before you buy. Or, if you can't replace a purchase you already made, carefully trim the offending knobs until they no longer rub the frame.

When riding with the wide rims and tires, you can run your air pressure much lower than the inflation that's recommended on the sidewall without getting a pinch flat. This will add to the flotation and make the ride softer. Check your tire pressure before each ride.

Brakes When Using Wide Rims

If you have disc brakes, you'll have no troubles with wider rims. Also, you'll have more reliable braking power than with rim-type brakes, especially when riding through fresh snow or water.

If you have direct-pull (V-type brakes), you will have to modify your setup to accommodate the wider rims. Take the bike to your favorite shop for advice on using rim brakes with wide rims.

Braking Power

The largest threat to braking power when using rim-type brakes in the cold is ice buildup on the rims. You can take steps to prevent the buildup from happening. Fresh snow will stick to warm metal, so before you ride set the bicycle out in the cold and let the rims cool down. (Be sure to lock it to prevent theft!) If you ride through water, pull on both brake levers while continuing to pedal. This will help sweep the water off the rims. If you can keep your rims clean and dry, you should have good braking.

Wet rims are why many winter cyclists turn to disc brakes, which are more reliable in wet conditions because the braking surface is farther away from the puddles.

Specialty Bikes

Bike manufacturers are slowly beginning to build frames for winter conditions. Wildfire Designs in Palmer builds FatBikes, snow bikes used in winter bike races. They are custom built to accommodate 80 mm rims, almost twice the width of the SnowCats. Talk to Wildfire Designs if you decide you want to delve into competitive snow racing. The bikes are also favored by some people for biking on sand. Some Lower 48 manufacturers are also entering the market with frames that accommodate the wider rims. Yet it is a small market of people who will brave the elements on two wheels. Check with local shops to see which models are available.

Lights

Although not needed during much of the summer months, a reliable headlight and flashing taillight are necessities during the winter because of the short daylight hours. On the shortest day of the year, around December 21, Anchorage sees a mere 5½ hours of sunlight, provided the sky isn't overcast. Inexpensive headlights that use disposable batteries are available, but a rechargeable system, while more expensive, projects more light, is more convenient and is less wasteful. A headlight and red taillight are required by law for anyone bicycling on a road after dark. Headlight models are available for the helmet or for mounting on the handlebar. Most taillights have a flashing mode, which stands out better.

A handlebar-mounted light points to where the bike is going and keeps the weight off your head. A helmet-mounted light allows riders to see off the side of the trail when they hear a noise, and it's helpful when doing a repair or when riding on twisting trails. On very dark nights, when there's little or no snow, two lights give you the best of both worlds: you can look into the woods around you while still keeping the trail ahead lit.

Dealing with the Elements

There is always a risk of hypothermia in Alaska, even when biking in the summer. Obviously, that risk is much greater in winter when temperatures dip below zero, the days are much shorter and conditions can change in a matter of hours. When cycling in the cold, you should always be prepared by carrying extra gear, including a windbreaker or dry fleece jacket, spare socks and gloves, and some high-energy food.

What to Wear

Riders should always be prepared to stay out longer than planned in case they get turned around, have to push through deep snow or have to stop to make a repair. When riding with a group, be prepared to stop more often, especially if people are of different skill levels or travel at different speeds. A rule of thumb for any group outing: the more riders, the more frequent the stops.

Dressing in layers, using breathable wind-blocking fabrics as your outer layer, is one of the best ways to regulate your temperature as you ride. (If you ride in the rain, the outer layer should also be waterproof.) Look for pants and tops that use wind-block fabric for the front of the body and a more breathable fabric for the back. Under heavy exertion, they allow the extra heat and moisture to leave the body. If you ride more moderately, you may want outer layers that are completely windproof and still breathable.

High-quality wools or synthetics are the best materials to wear, but each individual has his or her own preferences. Some people use vapor barriers to prevent body moisture from contaminating the middle layer. When clothes get wet, you'll lose heat faster. "Secrets of Warmth" by Hal Weiss has more detailed information on how the body loses heat and on ways to prevent it. It includes detailed discussions on layering techniques, including vapor barriers, and clothing materials.

Some keys to remember are these:

Avoid cotton. It holds moisture longer, and through the process of drying pulls heat away from your skin.

Use clothing that is windproof and breathable. This keeps the wind off but allows excess moisture to escape. In rainy conditions, use an outer layer that is waterproof and breathable.

Dress in layers. This allows you to add or remove one item to help regulate your temperature. If you're wearing just a thin base layer and a thick down coat, you have no middle ground—you're either too hot or too cold. With base, middle and top layers, you'll stay comfortable longer.

Keeping the extremities from frostbite or frost nip is a big challenge for bikers, but a few innovations and creativity will keep you from having problems with your feet and hands. Remember that a solution that works for one person may not work for everyone. Try different combinations of clothing, shoes, gloves and head coverings on shorter rides before setting off on a daylong excursion. One rule of thumb for biking and other active winter sports is to start out comfortably cool, neither warm nor cold. Once you get moving, you'll warm up. If you start out warm, you'll be shedding layers right away. On the other hand, if you don't warm up in the first five or 10 minutes, you should add a layer.

Prevention is the best way to ward off cold-related injuries, but you should also take time to learn about cold-weather first aid. Books are available at outdoor-oriented retail stores and bookshops.

Feet

Keeping the feet warm is one of the most challenging and critical problems faced by winter cyclists. Many riders who use clipless pedals in the summer turn to toe straps and hiking boots or felt-lined Sorrels in the winter. These keep the feet warm, but they take away the ability to use clipless pedals. Plus, the taller boots are cumbersome and don't allow any ankle movement. Riders who stay with clipless pedals and merely use thicker socks in their summer shoes find their shoes become too tight, reducing circulation. In addition, the rapid heat loss to the cleat can cause intense pain in the sole of the foot.

In recent years manufacturers have begun making winter riding shoes. They have a thicker insole, so less heat is lost into the cleat. They have a higher top with a flexible cuff to keep the snow out and are insulated. Leather models can be treated to be made waterproof.

While these work well for short rides, some endurance riders find that the shoes work best when purchased two or three sizes too big, to allow for thicker or multiple socks. Other riders use oversized summer biking shoes and replace the insoles with wool felt insoles. Windproof, insulated shoe covers can keep feet warmer on the coldest days.

Inside the shoes, you can wear a waterproof oversock layered over wool or high-loft synthetic socks. Some people swear by the vapor barrier method: a thin synthetic layer, followed by the vapor barrier sock, then a wool or high-loft synthetic sock. Try different combinations to find out what works best for you. Be sure to bring these sock layers when shopping for shoes.

If your choice of footwear still allows your feet to get cold, dismount and run with the bike to increase circulation. If possible, loosen the closures on your shoes. Go someplace warm and on another day try a different setup. Consider using chemical toe warmers or carrying them for emergencies.

Tip

Sometimes the trickiest part of ice riding is getting on and off the bicycle on icy streets and parking lots. For icy conditions, insert short sheet-metal screws into the bottom of each shoe; five per shoe should be enough to prevent a fall.

Hands

One of the best innovations for riding in very cold temperatures is handlebar poagies. Installed on each end of the handlebar, they look like sleeping bags for your hands. Poagies allow riders to wear lighter gloves, thereby keeping more dexterity for shifting and braking. They come in pairs and leave room on the center of the handlebar for equipment such as a headlamp or handlebar bag. Look for poagies that are waterproof and large enough to cover the bar ends. Riders should still carry a warmer pair of gloves in case of an emergency.

For riders not using poagies, heavier cycling gloves have been available for several years. You can also use ski gloves or those made for snowboarding or mountaineering. Remember that mittens, because they keep your fingers together, are warmer than gloves. The toughest part of using the heavier gloves and mittens is they make it difficult to use trigger-style shifters. Consider using a twist-style shifter for your winter riding.

Head

Some riders are tempted to forgo wearing their helmet in the winter, but a slip on the ice could very easily leave them unconscious and exposed to the elements. Often the reason they don't use a helmet is that it won't fit over their hat. There are several solutions, including wearing a thin ear band or a thin skullcap designed to go under the helmet. Some ski hats are also thin enough. Balaclavas designed for biking work well and provide face coverage. Another option is to wear a hooded synthetic top, which also gives good neck coverage. If these don't work, you could get a larger helmet for winter riding.

Many newer helmets are designed with vents to keep riders cool in the summer. A simple winter adjustment is to cover the vents with tape or use a helmet cover. Unfortunately, most helmet covers don't allow for a helmet-mounted headlamp, so that would require modification. A less ventilated helmet, such as one designed for BMX riding, will be warmer and have more padding and coverage. Not all have holes for a headlamp, so watch for this feature. A winter helmet should be adjustable for different hat thickness and fit well.

Eye Covering

Just like in the summer, it's a good idea to wear eye protection. Eyewear will protect you from injuries from overhanging branches or snow and gravel flying up from your wheel or the wheel of a riding partner. They can prevent damage from the cold and can help riders see the trail better. Sunglasses with interchangeable colored lenses allow riders to use specific lenses for different conditions; yellow or gold lenses help bring out contours in the trails on low-light days. Ski goggles are also popular when the temperature really takes a dive.

Water and Food

Even in winter, you lose fluids when exercising. But because it's not warm outside, you may forget to keep hydrated. People burn more energy in winter just keeping the body warm, so it's important to have food on hand. The challenges are in preventing the water from freezing and in having food that is easy to eat.

Water Bottle

If you mount a water bottle on your bike, place it upside down in the bottle cage—since ice floats, it won't form as quickly in the cap. Start with warm water so it takes longer to freeze. A bottle with a twist-off cap is easier to open with heavy gloves than one with a flip cap if the nozzle does freeze.

Hydration Packs

When using a hydration-type backpack, wear it inside your top layer to keep the water warm. Start with warm water. After drinking, blow the water left in the drinking tube back into the bladder. Once the water freezes in the line, it's impossible to get a drink without opening the bladder. Insulated packs and upgrade kits are available for the drinking tube, but many of those on the market aren't sufficient for the coldest days in Alaska. Some people use foam pipe insulation wrapped in duct tape. It's bulky but light and worth trying.

Food

Winter biking takes more energy than summer riding, especially if you have to pedal or push through fresh snow. Bring food that won't freeze and is easy to handle. If you're using a hydration pack for your water, fill a water bottle with trail mix and place it in your bottle cage. Just remove the cap and pour the contents directly into your mouth (a screw-top bottle works best). Often commercial energy bars will freeze so hard they are difficult, if not impossible, to eat. Cut them into pieces beforehand and put them in a bottle or a zip-type sandwich bag. Stash the bag in an easily accessible inner pocket to keep it from freezing. A simple peanut butter and jelly sandwich also makes great energy food and is easy to handle when cut into pieces.

Where to Ride

On your first few winter bike rides, you'll learn what works and what doesn't work with your gear setup. Soon you'll come to understand and appreciate the draw of winter cycling. Maybe it's discovering, then trusting, the traction you get from studded tires as you cruise across a frozen pond. Maybe it's the pleasure of hearing the snow crunching under your tires as you ride through the black and white of a birch forest, the crisp air void of smell.

Winter cycling may take hold of you and you'll want to explore every route possible. Below is a list of trails open to cyclists during the winter. Remember, any trails that are groomed for skiing-only are off-limits to cyclists. If you see a sign that says "No dogs on groomed ski trails" or similar wording, consider it off-limits to you on your bike. On multi-use routes that are groomed for skiing, avoid riding on a freshly groomed surface, since it takes two to four hours for the surface to set up. And, by all means, don't ride on the parallel tracks set for classic skiers.

You must also stay off the dog mushing trails during the winter. Dog teams travel quite fast (up to 30 miles per hour) and need a long distance to stop. Stay alert at trail crossings, which are usually marked, so you don't collide with a team. If it is a poor snow year with just ice on the mushing trails, the dogs probably won't be running. In these conditions, if the ice is thick, you can sometimes bike the mushing trails. Watch for open water and learn to recognize the characteristics of thin ice. For safety, ride with a partner and leave a few bike lengths between riders on routes that cover ponds and marshes.

People are still getting used to seeing cyclists riding during the winter, but cyclists have a right to use the winter trails. Remember that following the rules will lead to more acceptance. Trails that are designated multi-use are open to ride; remember to yield to other users, just as you do during the summer.

Winter Biking Routes

2-1   Tony Knowles Coastal Trail
2-2   Lanie Fleischer Chester Creek Trail
2-3   Campbell Creek Trail
2-4   Connecting the Campbell Creek and Chester Creek Trails
2-6   Russian Jack Springs—paved route only.
4-4   Abbott Trail and Gasline Multi-Use Corridor
4-6   Rover's Run, Moose Meadow and Black Bear Trail (portions of route).
4-8   Tour of Anchorage (Viewpoint, Homestead, Old Rondy) route
4-9   Moose Track Trail
4-10 Coyote Trail
4-11 Lore Road Trail
4-13 Bulldog (Tank) Trail
4-14 Moose Ridge Loop and connecting skijor loops
5-3   Powerline Trail
7-2   Peters Creek Trail
7-3   Eklutna Lakeside Trail

Appendices

Ride Ratings by Difficulty

Easy

Ride #	Ride Name	Description	Surface
2-2	Lanie Fleischer Chester Creek Trail	Mostly level	Paved
2-3a	Cambpell Creek Trail West of Seward Hwy.	Mostly level	Paved
2-3b	Campbell Creek Trail Lake Otis Pkwy. to Tudor Road	Mostly level	Paved
2-3c	Campbell Creek Trail Lake Otis Parkway to Seward Hwy.	Level, some traffic crossings	Paved
2-4	Connecting the Campbell Creek and Chester Creek Trails	Level terrain	Paved, gravel
3-1	Jodhpur Loop	Wide, grassy	Dirt
4-2	Besh Loop	Wide, gravel	Gravel
4-3	Service Loop	Wide, gravel	Gravel
4-9	Moose Track Trail	Gravel, ADA trail	Gravel
7-1b	Beach Lake Nordic Ski Trails Green Trail	A few small hills	Dirt

Easy – Moderate

Ride #	Ride Name	Description	Surface
2-1	Tony Knowles Coastal Trail	Distance	Paved
2-5	University Area Mahaffey Trails	Hills	Dirt
2-6	Russian Jack Springs Park	Off-road portion	Paved, dirt
2-7	Glenn Highway Trail	Distance	Paved
3-5	Raspberry Parking Lot to Stadium via Margaux's Loop	Some hills, blind corners	Dirt
3-6	Stadium to Raspberry Parking Lot via Margaux's Loop	Some steep hills	Dirt
3-9	Mize Loop	Some hills	Dirt
3-10	Sisson Loop	Steep to enter and exit route	Dirt

Easy – Moderate

Ride #	Ride Name	Description	Surface
4-1	Hillside Loop	Hills	Gravel
4-4	Abbott Road Multi-Use Trail	Some hills	Dirt
4-8a	Tour of Anchorage (Homestead/Viewpoint Trails)	One steep hill	Gravel, dirt
4-8b	Tour of Anchorage (Old Rondy Trail) continued	Some narrow wet sections	Gravel, dirt
4-10	Coyote Trail	Can be muddy	Dirt
4-11	Lore Road Trail	Some narrow sections	Dirt
4-13	Bulldog Trail (also known as the Tank Trail)	Distance	Gravel
6-1	Indian to Bird to Girdwood	Due to wind, distance, hills	Paved
7-3	Eklutna Lakeside Trail	Distance	Gravel, dirt

Moderate

3-2	Horseshoe Loop	Somewhat steep	Dirt
3-7	Lake Loop from Margaux's Loop	Steep climbs and descents	Dirt
3-8	Inner Lake Loop	Hills	Dirt
5-1	Near Point	Some rocks, water bar	Gravel, dirt
7-1a	Beach Lake Nordic Ski Trails Red Trail	Some loose sand and rocks, hills	Dirt
7-2	Peters Creek Trail	Long climb, water crossings, some singletrack	Gravel, dirt

Moderate–Difficult

2-8	Arctic Valley Road Hill Climb	Sustained gravel climb	Gravel road
3-3	Ice Box, Hair Pin, Mize's Folly, The Wall	Steep hills, loose sand	Dirt

Moderate-Difficult

Ride #	Ride Name	Description	Surface
3-4	Big Dipper, Stairway to Heaven, Compression	Steep hills	Dirt
3-11	Lekisch Trail	Steep, loose sand	Dirt
4-5	Richter and Ridge Loops	Steep hills, rooty	Dirt
4-6	Rover's Run, Moose Meadow, and Black Bear Trail	Steep hills, singletrack, roots	Dirt
4-7	Spencer Loop, including Double Bubble	Long climbs, twisty descents	Dirt
4-12	Balto Loop	Singletrack roots, ruts	Dirt
4-14	Moose Ridge Loop	Singletrack, few signs	Dirt
4-15	Dogwood Trail	Singletrack, no signs	Dirt
5-3a	Prospect Heights to Glen Alps (Powerline Trail)	Strenuous climb, waterbars	Dirt, gravel
5-3b	Upper Huffman to Glen Alps (Powerline Trail)	Steep grades	Dirt, gravel
5-3c	Glen Alps to Powerline Out-and-Back riders	Steep climb and descent, loose rocks, creek crossing	Gravel

Difficult

Ride #	Ride Name	Description	Surface
5-2	Upper Gasline Trail	Very steep, large loose rocks	Gravel
5-3c	Glen Alps to Indian (Powerline Trail)	Very steep, off-camber, large loose rocks, creek crossings	Gravel, dirt
6-2	Alyeska downhill trails	Steep, off-camber, loose with obstacles	Dirt

Resources

Anchorage-Area Bike Shops

Some area shops offer rentals or demos.

Alaska Mountain Bike Source
2375 East 63rd Avenue
Anchorage 99507
(907) 245-8844
www.alaskamtnbike.com
Rentals and demos available.

The Bike Department at The Motorcycle Shop
400 West Potter Drive
Anchorage 99518
(907) 561-1131

The Bicycle Exchange
2601 Barrow Street
Anchorage 99503
(907) 276-2453
Rentals available.

The Bicycle Shop
1035 West Northern Lights Boulevard
Anchorage 99503
(907) 272-5219

Girdwood Ski & Cyclery
Mile 1.5 Alyeska Highway
Girdwood 99587
(907) 783-2453
Rentals available.

Paramount Cycles
1320 Huffman Park Drive
Anchorage 99515
(907) 336-2453

Pat's Bikes
6921 Brayton Drive, Suite 200
Anchorage 99507
(907) 770-6560
www.patsbikeshop.com
Demos available.

RTR Bicycles—Ready to Race
3110 East 42nd Avenue
Anchorage 99508
(907) 563-2054

Recreational Equipment Inc. (REI)
1200 West Northern Lights Boulevard
Anchorage 99503
(907) 272-4565

Sunshine Sports
1231 West Northern Lights Boulevard
Anchorage 99503
(907) 272-6444
Rentals available.

Wildfire Designs
824 South Colony Way
Palmer 99645
(907) 745-2453
www.wildfirecycles.com

Rentals

Downhill Division at Alyeska Resort

PO Box 1177
Girdwood 99587
(907) 230-3437
warren@akadventures.net
Downhill bikes available for use onsite.

Downtown Bicycle Rental

333 West 4th Avenue, Suite 206
Anchorage 99501
(907) 279-5293
www.alaska-bike-rentals.com

Lifetime Adventures

(Eklutna Lake)
PO Box 1205
Palmer 99645
(907) 746-4644
www.lifetimeadventures.net
Bicycle and kayak rentals.

Land Managers and Information

Alaska Public Lands Information Center (APLIC)

605 West 4th Avenue, Suite 105
Anchorage 99501
(907) 271- 2737
www.nps.gov/aplic

Anchorage Parks & Recreation Department

PO Box 196650
Anchorage 99519-6650
www.muni.org/parks

- **Main office**,
  (907) 343-4474
  120 South Bragaw Street
  (corner of Bragaw and Mountain View Drive)

- **Kincaid Chalet**,
  (907) 343-6397

- **Eagle River**,
  (907) 694-2011

- **Girdwood**, (907) 783-1006

- **Street & Park Maintenance Dispatch**,
  (907) 343-8277

Anchorage Ski Club, Inc.

PO Box 102571
Anchorage 99510-2571
(907) 428-1208
www.skialpenglow.com
Maintains facilities and provides access to Chugach State Park from Arctic Valley Road.

Bureau of Land Management Campbell Creek Science Center

6881 Abbott Loop Road
Anchorage 99507-2599
(907) 267-1245 www.anchorage.ak.blm.gov/ccscentr.html

Chugach State Park
Potter Section House
HC 52 Box 8999
Indian 99540
(907) 345-5014
www.alaskastateparks.org

Fort Richardson

* Natural resources officer, (907) 384-2744
* Conservation enforcement officer, (907) 384-3175

To legally access any trails on Fort Richardson, you must first get a recreation access permit (RAP). To obtain the permit, go to the main gate at Fort Richardson, present your identification and fill out a form. The permit is valid for that calendar year only.

After getting the permit, check in using the USAR-TRAK (U.S. Army Garrison Alaska Recreation Tracking System) phone access system. The system will tell you which areas are off-limits to recreational use at that time. Remember to check out after leaving the military land.

It's not necessary to phone into the system if you are riding Arctic Valley Road, but if you plan to leave the road, you must call in. Each person in a group must have a permit and check in separately.

Directions to main gate: Drive north from Anchorage on the Glenn Highway. Drive 2.9 miles past the Muldoon overpass and take the Fort Richardson exit. (This is also the second exit for Arctic Valley Road.) Turn left to cross the highway and arrive at the main gate.

Fort Rich is revising its policy regarding the carrying and use of weapons in the Bulldog (Tank) Trail area. Check with the Conservation Enforcement Officer before taking any weapon onto the post.

Hilltop Ski Area
7015 Abbott Road
Anchorage 99507
(907) 346-1446
www.hilltopskiarea.org

Bicycle Clubs

Arctic Bicycle Club
PO Box 230130
Anchorage 99523-0130
Hotline: (907) 566-0177
www.arcticbike.org

Singletrack Advocates (STA)
PO Box 240574
Anchorage 99524
www.singletrackadvocates.org

Susitna Communities Active Bicyclists Society (SCABS)
PO Box 810
Willow 99688
(907) 733-2878
monksown@hotmail.com

Valley Mountain Bike Alliance
824 South Colony Way
Palmer 99645
(907) 745-2453
wildfire@mtaonline.net

WOMBATS—Women's Mountain Bike & Tea Society,
Anchorage Chapter
PO Box 232023
Anchorage 99523
www.wombats.org
anchoragewombats@yahoo.com

Other Clubs

Alaska Sled Dog & Racing Association (ASDRA)
PO Box 110569
Anchorage 99511
907-562-2235
www.asdra.org

Anchorage Trails and Greenways Coalition
PO Box 92394
Anchorage 99509
907-566-2842

Arctic Orienteering Club Inc.
PO Box 241003
Anchorage 99524-1003
www.alaska.net/~oalaska
Has links to numerous running groups.

Nordic Skiing Association of Anchorage (NSAA)
203 West 15th Avenue, Suite 204
Anchorage 99501
(907) 276-7609
Trails hotline: 907-248-6667
www.anchoragenordicski.com

North American Skijoring and Ski Pulk Association (NASSPA)
PO Box 240573
Anchorage 99524
Hotline: (907) 349-9663
www.ptialaska.net/~skijor

Further Reading

Several hiking guides for the south-central part of the state can be found in bookshops and outdoor specialty stores. Other resources on topics relating to the area include:

Field Guide to Alaskan Wildflowers, by Verna E. Pratt

Guidebook to Geology of Anchorage, Alaska, by Lorie M. Dilley, P.E., C.P.G., and Thomas E. Dilley, Ph.D.

A Naturalist's Guide to Chugach State Park, by Jenny Zimmerman

Secrets of Warmth for Comfort or Survival, by Hal Weiss

Snow Sense: A Guide to Evaluating Snow Avalanche Hazard, by Jill A. Fredston and Doug Fesler

Wheels on Ice: Bicycling in Alaska 1898–1908, edited by Terrence Cole (out of print)

Numerous publications address traveling and living in bear country. Some recommend not mountain biking in bear country. Because all of Anchorage is bear country, however, it's best to learn how to behave in order to avoid a dangerous encounter. Some helpful information is on these government websites:

www.wildlife.alaska.gov/aawildlife/ak_bears.cfm

www.dnr.state.ak.us/parks/safety/bears.htm

www.wildlife.alaska.gov/aawildlife/bearfax.cfm (The text at this site was excerpted and adapted from a brochure, "Bear Facts," produced by Alaska Department of Fish & Game, in cooperation with other state and federal agencies.)

www.audubon.org/chapter/ak/ak/index.htm (Includes the downloadable book: Living in Harmony with Bears, published by the National Audubon Society, Alaska State Office)

Glossary

bollard – a barrier post at a trailhead that prevents vehicles from entering the trail.

bonk – to suddenly lose energy, usually due to not eating enough or not eating high-energy foods.

breakup – the period of spring when the snow melts rapidly; also refers to when the ice flows out of some rivers. The time of year when it's most critical to stay off the natural-surface trails to prevent damage.

cow parsnip – sometimes known as pootschki, this broad-leafed plant grows up to 8 feet tall with sprawling leaves and white flowers. Contact with the leaves or stems, especially on sunny days, can cause severe blisters that are slow to heal and can leave scarring.

cyclocross or cross bike – a road-style bike outfitted for use on dirt trails with larger, knobby tires and other modifications. Can be used on paved routes and hard-packed dirt trails.

full-suspension – a mountain bike with shocks on the fork and the rear triangle.

hardtail – a mountain bike with shocks on the fork.

hybrid – a bike with 700 cm wheels and a mountain-style frame. Can be used on paved routes, but tires often are slick, so they're not ideal for off-road riding.

iron ranger – a metal self-pay station where trail users may deposit their fees. Used at the state park trailheads.

line – the most heavily used route on a trail, particularly on a wider grass-surface trail. Can also refer to the route between two points.

mogul – a bump in the trail. Some would ride around it; others will launch off it.

multi-use – a trail open to a variety of users at the same time, as opposed to a single-use trail. The distinction is particularly important during winter.

singletrack – a trail so narrow that users must generally travel single file.

skijor – a Norwegian term meaning "ski-driving"; refers to cross-country skiing using one or two dogs as draft animals. Pronounced ski-jur.

snowmachine – Alaska term for snowmobile; also refered to as a snow-go.

trail corridor – the cleared area on both sides of the tread or line; the area through which the trail runs.

trailhead – the beginning point of a trail.

tread – the trail surface on which bikers ride.

water bar – a structure that diverts water off to the side of a trail. Usually made of wood or rock.

whoop-de-do – terrain that undulates repeatedly in a short distance.

Index

Trail Notes

Trail Notes

Trail Notes

Trail Notes

_____
_____
_____
_____
_____
_____
_____
_____
_____
_____
_____
_____
_____
_____
_____
_____
_____
_____
_____
_____
_____
_____
_____
_____
_____
_____
_____
_____
_____
_____
_____

Trail Notes

Trail Notes